The Fundamentals of
Segmented Woodturning

The Fundamentals of
Segmented Woodturning

*Projects, Techniques & Innovations
for Today's Woodturner*

James Rodgers

LINDEN PUBLISHING
FRESNO

The Fundamentals of Segmented Woodturning
Projects, Techniques & Innovations for Today's Woodturner
by
James Rodgers

© James Rodgers 2016
Cover design by Jim Goold
Interior design and layout by Maura J. Zimmer

ISBN: 978-1-610352-78-9
35798642

Linden Publishing titles may be purchased in quantity at special discounts for educational, business, or promotional use. To inquire about discount pricing, please refer to the contact information below. For permission to use any portion of this book for academic purposes, please contact the Copyright Clearance Center at www.copyright.com

Printed in the United States of America

Library of Congress Cataloging-in-Publication Data

Names: Rodgers, James, 1941 November 16- author.
Title: The fundamentals of segmented woodturning : projects, techniques & innovations for today's woodturner / James Rodgers.
Description: Fresno : Linden Publishing, Inc., [2016]
Identifiers: LCCN 2016031653 | ISBN 9781610352789 (pbk. : alk. paper)
Subjects: LCSH: Turning (Lathe work)--Handbooks, manuals, etc. | Woodwork--Handbooks, manuals, etc.
Classification: LCC TT203 .R64 2016 | DDC 684/.08--dc23
LC record available at https://lccn.loc.gov/2016031653

Linden Publishing, Inc.
2006 S. Mary
Fresno, CA 93721
www.lindenpub.com

Acknowledgements

In creating this book I have had help from several sources without which I could not have done the project:

First my proof reader without whom the publisher would have had an impossible task, Sharon Rodgers, my wife.

Ron Kersey taught me how to use SketchUp for my last book and helped solve several technical drawing problems in this book; we both learned even more.

Jerry Jakubowski, a friend and former student, read, critiqued, and offered substantive recommendations in formatting and presentation.

Lastly to all my current and former students in the classroom and on line for their help in clarifying processes and their encouragement to undertake this work.

Thanks to all.

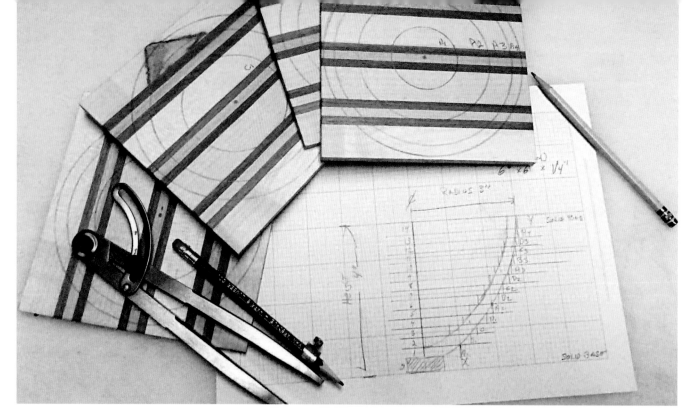

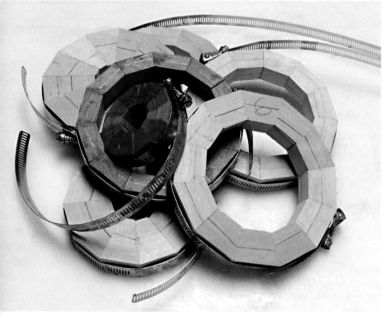

Contents

Preface

Drawings

In the book the author has used drawings of half bowls and vessels to illustrate the measurements and calculations. Many turners prefer to make half form drawings as it is easier. The calculations are exactly the same whether you work from diameter or radii.

Measurements

Measurements are in fractional inches, the most commonly used measurement system in the United States and woodturning in particular. Unfortunately, the process of converting fractions to decimal inches, multiplying by another decimal (usually π or 3.14) then estimating the conversion back to fractions is tedious. The simplest measurement system to

use is the metric system where no conversions are required and division of a measurement is straight forward. I encourage you to consider conversion to metric.

All commercial software used in segmented turning can be set to fractional inches, decimal inches, or metric measurements. When building your fixtures consider adding measuring tapes with metric measurements.

Theory and Practice

Each chapter consists of two parts: the explanation of the concept and an example to make in practice. The author has used graphics in the initial theory, and assembly pictures in the second section to further aid in clarity.

Information on specific accessories and fixture construction plans can be found at the web sites referenced in the appendix.

Cautions: Remember that woodturning can be dangerous if safety precautions are not observed including wearing eye and face protection, keeping your tools sharp and following all manufacturer's safety precautions. The techniques and power tools usage presented in this book are the ones most used by the author over many years of teaching segmentation techniques and which he finds the easiest to initially assimilate.

Introduction

The emphasis on segmentation has grown, expanding in new directions and adding new processes. This book gives the new segmenter a simple introduction, new avenues to explore, and techniques to try. The approach of this book is intended to be more visual than written where possible.

Ring segmented vessel

Why Segmented Woodturning?

With segmented techniques many unique vessels can be created by selection of wood, design and assembly techniques. The choices in designs are limitless. You can find a great board at the local woodworking dealer and know that you can make a bowl or vessel without spending a small fortune for the materials. You use standard woodworking techniques to create cuts with precision and woodturning techniques to complete your projects.

What is Segmented Woodturning?

Segmented wood turning is the process of building from flat stock by cutting, arranging and gluing interesting woods into more complex, and beautiful projects.

Ring segmented turning is the process of building segmented rings, stacking them into bowls or vessels, and turning the shape by traditional methods. By choosing wood species of various colors and textures elaborate designs can be developed and woven into the fabric of the vessel.

Open segment turning requires space between the individual segments. Indexing is required to get the proper spacing between the segments. This technique requires less precise cutting but more care in the assembly of the project.

Bowls from a board assemblies start with a laminated, multicolored board. They are then sliced into rings, stacked, rotated and turned. The beauty is in the apparent complexity. While the assembly is not complicated more attention is given to designing and planning of the project.

Open segment vessel

Bowl from a board

Stave segmented vessel

Chapter 3, Building a Hollow Vessel takes you another step forward with a process for working with closed containers using a two face plate method. A few more tips on the basics are also included.

Chapter 4, Simple Design Enhancements adds some enhancements that will dress up any project with little additional effort.

Chapter 5, Techniques for Making Feature Rings presents you with techniques that can be used to create more complex designs using cutting, sanding and glue up procedures. With these techniques you can attain very complex patterns of your own design.

Stave segmented turning is dealing with very tall segmented rings or staves. The tall stave segments can be cut the length of the planned project or at compound angles to reduce material usage. This technique will not be covered in this book.

Layout of this book
This book covers the basics of each technique, enough to get you started.

Chapter 1, Getting Started— How It's Done covers the steps of a construction where you will learn the basics.

Chapter 2, Cutting Segments Accurately presents four different segment cutting techniques and where they may be applied.

Chapter 6, Setting Up and Building an Open Segment Vessel introduces you to techniques and fixtures required to place individual segments in projects where ring techniques won't work.

Chapter 7, Bowl from a Board presents lamination, cutting and re-assembly techniques for building mind blowing "dizzy bowl" projects.

Chapters 8 and 9, Segmented Pens & Transitional Vessels covers some fun techniques, simple and fast ideas for scrap-based projects. These are quick and can be done in a limited amount of spare time.

What you will need

It is important to have the woodworking tools necessary to true, square and thickness the lumber you purchase so that when you process it into segments they will be as accurate as possible.

Cutting segments accurately and repeatedly requires a sled fitted to your table saw or miter saw. It must allow you to make the same cut many times safely and with precision. The number of segments required will determine the angle of the cut.

Checking and adjusting the flatness of the construction at each assembly stage requires a bright light, a straight edge and a flat sanding stick. A wide-belt thickness sander is nice to have but not required.

To allow assemblies to be moved without loss of alignment will require a lot of faceplate/glue block assemblies, which provide more precision than the use of a scroll chuck.

Band clamps or rubber bands are needed to clamp the rings tightly while the glue dries.

A sanding disk used on the lathe, a disk sander or thickness sander (not a planer—it won't work) is needed to flatten the face of rings before gluing in order to get tight joints. The disc sander is also a major accessory for many feature ring designs.

Aligning rings during assembly requires centering—cones, jumbo jaws, or even a Vernier caliper will do the job.

For open segment construction an accurate indexing method and a fixture to position each segment during the glue up is needed.

Terms Used in This Book

Segment: A segment *(Figure 1)* is the basic component cut from

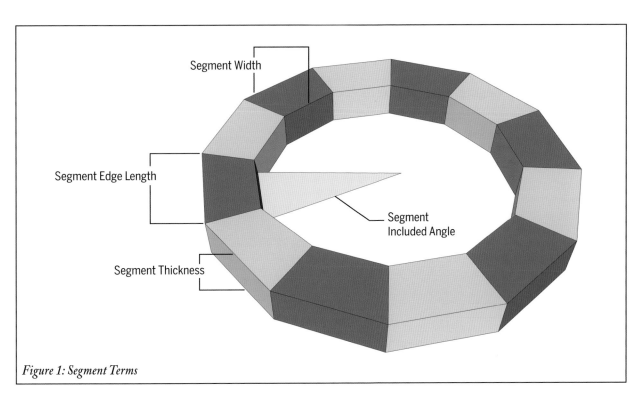

Segment Width

Segment Edge Length

Segment Thickness

Segment Included Angle

Figure 1: Segment Terms

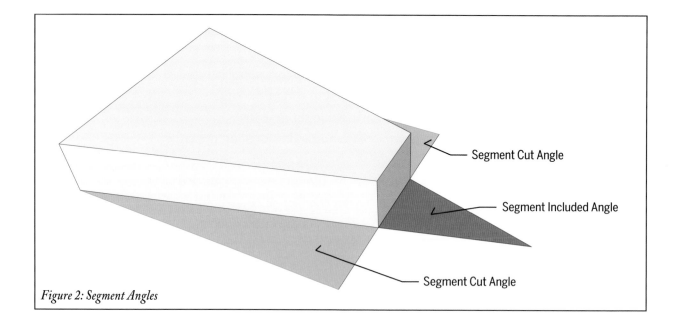

Segment Cut Angle

Segment Included Angle

Segment Cut Angle

Figure 2: Segment Angles

a prepared strip of timber. It has three dimensions:

Segment Thickness: The thickness of the stock when cut into a segment will be the height of the layer being constructed.

Segment Width: The width of the strip from which the segment is cut which will become the wall thickness for the project.

Segment Edge Length: The outside width of the segment that determines the outside diameter of the ring being constructed.

Segment Included Angle/Cut Angle: *(Figure 2)* The included angle is 360 degrees (the number of degrees in a circle) divided by the number of segments in the ring being constructed. On some cutting sleds one half of the segment's included angle is set; the segment has one side cut, the strip flipped and the second side is cut. This set angle is referred to as the segment cut angle; on other cutting sleds the segment included angle is set.

Getting Started, How It's Done— The Basic Steps

1

Cautions:

- Always plan ahead, build a cutting plan and follow it.
- Assure that woods used are dry and stable.
- Build grain alignment into your plans.
- Make clean, tight joints.

Start with a simple bowl where you can follow the basic steps of ring segmentation and build a project at the same time.

Make a Drawing

Make a full-scale drawing on graph paper with a wall thickness of at least ½". *(Figure 1)*

Determine the thickness of each ring to be built which may be the thickness of the wood you purchased such as ¾" stock. Add horizontal lines to your drawing to indicate that thickness; number each level. *(Figure 2)*

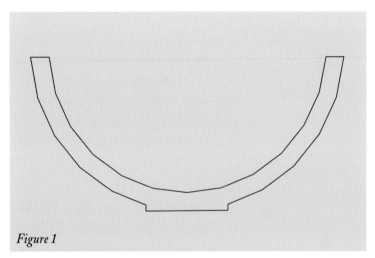

Figure 1

A basic bowl drawing with an interior wall added

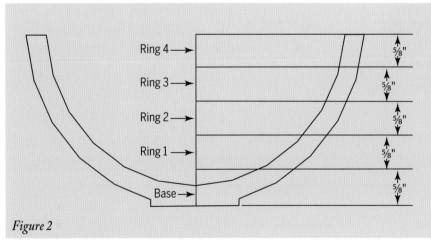

Figure 2

Drawing with layers indicated and numbered

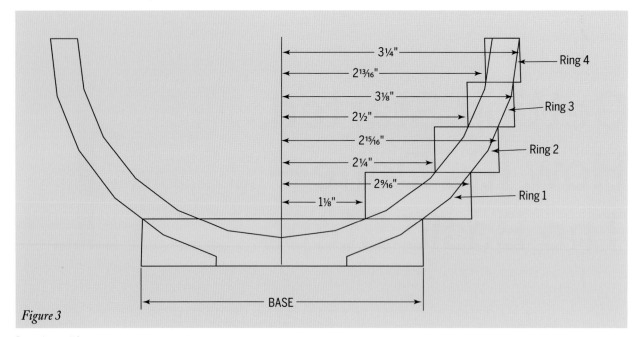

Figure 3

Drawing with the min/max radii recorded on the drawing

For each level mark the widest exterior radius and the narrowest interior radius and record those dimensions on the drawing. *(Figure 3)*

Build a Cut List

Calculate the stock length required by multiplying the maximum radius of each ring level by 2π (3.14 x 2) to get the circumference of that ring; add five additional inches. This additional material allows for the 12 separate ⅛" saw kerfs from cutting the segments, additional material for replacing errors and enough for holding safely while cutting. Start a chart and record this information as the required material length. *(Cut List 1)*

Subtract each layer's minimum radius from its maximum radius and record this as the stock width for that ring. *(Cut List 2)*

Calculate the segment edge length by dividing the circumference of each ring (2 π x radius) by the number of segments desired for the project and record this as the segment edge length. In this example we are building a bowl with 12 segments to each ring. *(Cut List 3)*

Divide the number of segments into 360 (number of degrees in a circle) and record this as the segment's included angle. *(Cut List 4)*

There are several software programs on the market that can assist with the vessel drawing, completing the calculations and providing a printable cut list. These programs utilize trigonometry to accurately calculate the dimensions taking into account both vertical and horizontal curvatures that our simple "flat" graph paper cannot do. Check them out; a list of sources is in the appendix.

Cut List 1: Table with stock length calculated and added

LAYER	Circumference	Stock/Ring Thickness	Stock Length				
Ring 4	20.4"	⅝"	25½"				
Ring 3	19.6"	⅝"	24½"				
Ring 2	18.8"	⅝"	24"				
Ring 1	16.1"	⅝"	21"				
Base		⅝"	4"				

Cut List 2: Table with stock width dimensions added

LAYER	Circumference	Stock/Ring Thickness	Stock Length	Stock Width			
Ring 4	20.4"	⅝"	25"	⁷⁄₁₆"			
Ring 3	19.6"	⅝"	24"	⅝"			
Ring 2	18.8"	⅝"	23"	¹¹⁄₁₆"			
Ring 1	16.1"	⅝"	20"	⁷⁄₁₆"			
Base		⅝"	4"	4"			

Cut List 3: Table with segment included angle calculated and added

LAYER	Circumference	Stock/Ring Thickness	Stock Length	Stock Width	Number of Segments	Segment Edge Length	
Ring 4	20.4"	⅝"	25½"	⁷⁄₁₆"	12	1¹¹⁄₁₆"	
Ring 3	19.6"	⅝"	24½"	⅝"	12	1⅝"	
Ring 2	18.8"	⅝"	24"	¹¹⁄₁₆"	12	1⁹⁄₁₆"	
Ring 1	16.1"	⅝"	21"	⁷⁄₁₆"	12	1⁵⁄₁₆"	
Base		⅝"	4"	4"			

Cut List 4: Table with segment included angle calculated and added

LAYER	Circumference	Stock/Ring Thickness	Stock Length	Stock Width	Number of Segments	Segment Edge Length	Included/ Cut Angle
Ring 4	20.4"	⅝"	25½"	⁷⁄₁₆"	12	1¹¹⁄₁₆"	30°/15°
Ring 3	19.6"	⅝"	24½"	⅝"	12	1⅝"	30°/15°
Ring 2	18.8"	⅝"	24"	¹¹⁄₁₆"	12	1⁹⁄₁₆"	30°/15°
Ring 1	16.1"	⅝"	21"	⁷⁄₁₆"	12	1⁵⁄₁₆"	30°/15°
Base		⅝"	4"	4"			

1

Stock ripped
and cross cut for
making segments

Cut the Segments

Rip the stock to width and cross cut it to a length to exceed the material length needed from data in the table and number the strips to match each ring number. Also cut a square for the base. *(Photo 1)*

Crosscut the segments on your cutting sled and bag them to keep them sorted (the next chapter covers cutting accurate segments in detail). *(Photo 2)*

De-burr each segment being careful not to touch the cut faces. *(Photo 3)*

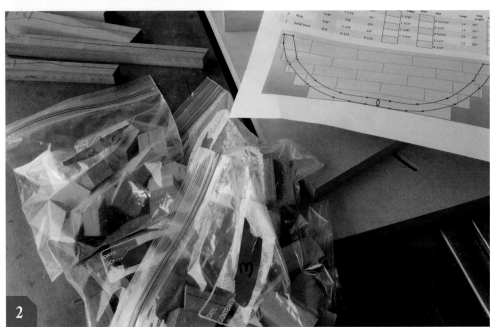

2

Cutting and
bagging segments

3

Deburring
the segments

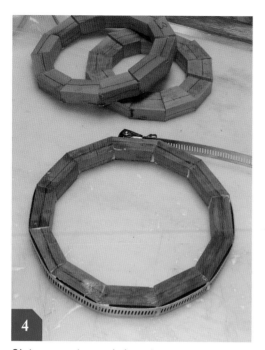

Gluing up a ring and clamping

Sanding one ring face flat

Prepare the Rings

On a flat glue surface, glue the segments together into rings using good quality PVA glue. Use metal hose clamps or rubber bands to secure the ring until the glue sets. *(Photo 4)*

Mark the ring number on each ring's edge and sand one face dead flat on a disk sander. If you own a thickness sander you may sand both faces flat and parallel. *(Photo 5)*

Build the Project

Mount a faceplate with a glue block on the lathe and flatten its face checking it with a straight edge and bright light. *(Photo 6)* When the assembly appears flat, no light shines between the lamp and a straight edge, sand it with a flat sanding stick.

Checking flatness of face plate/glue block assembly

Sanding the first ring glue up flat

Aligning the
second ring to the
rounded base

All bowl layers
glued up

Mount the solid base to the glue block with glue and when dry, flatten it again as you did in the step above. *(Photo 7)*

Add the first ring centering it carefully. After the glue dries, flatten the assembly and sand the exposed face. *(Photo 8)*

Mount the second ring carefully centering it on the first and rotating it to create a "brick laid" pattern. Continue to add rings and flatten until the full bowl is glued up. *(Photo 9)*

Turn and Complete the Bowl

Turn the exterior shape following your drawing. Turn from the rim down toward the base leaving the base area oversized for support. *(Photo 10)*

Turn the interior, working down from the top toward the base one level at a time completing the top ring before proceeding to the next lower level.

When the interior is completed reduce the base area to its final dimension adding a small parting cut at the bottom edge of the base. *(Photo 11)*

Sand and add an appropriate topcoat before parting off and finishing the base. *(Photo 12)*

Exterior rough turned

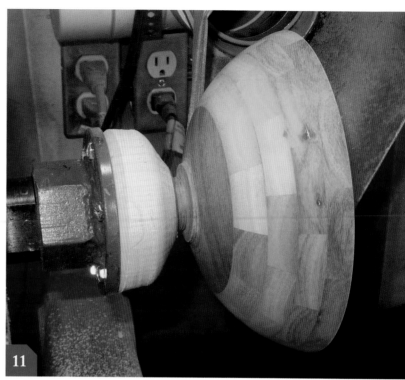

Reducing the base and adding a parting cut

The completed bowl, parted off and topcoated

2 Cutting Segments Accurately

Cutting segments is the most important part of segmentation. Accuracy, repeatability, precision, all start with the cutting fixture. Saw blades should be 60–80 tooth cross cut, full kerf blades. Your saw needs to be calibrated to assure the blade cuts straight and is exactly vertical to the table.

The Traditional Sled

The most frequently used cutting sled is built to cut a specific number of segments. One half of the segment's included angle is cut, the strip is flipped, and the second half is cut. With two cuts per segment, a 12 segment ring has 24 separate cuts and an opportunity of error at each cut. When a fixed-angle sled is

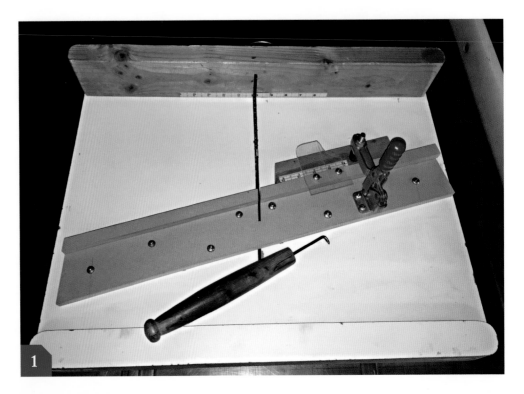

Traditional
Cutting Sled

1

constructed it must be carefully calibrated to create the highest degree of angular accuracy. After initial assembly, cut a test ring and check the fit. If there are any gaps, *(Photo 2)* adjust the fence until the gap on the next test ring disappears, and then carefully screw everything in place and you are ready to work.

The design pictured traps the cut segments for more rigidity; a segment hold down tool keeps the fingers away from the saw blade and holds the segment in place until the cut is completed. *(Photo 3)* This sled will maintain its accuracy from project to project because accuracy is built into the sled. A construction plan for this version is in the appendix and can be modified for any number of segments.

Its main features are:
- Fixed accuracy for a specific number of segments

2 Ring with gaps

- Support of the cut segment on both sides of the saw blade
- Ability to cut a segment from its center to each edge which is required in many feature ring designs
- Ability to easily recut or shorten segments

3 Using a segment hold down tool

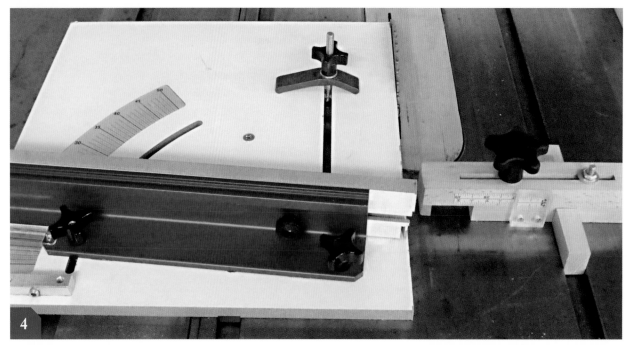

4

The Miter Sled with segment stop

The Miter Sled

The miter sled can be set at any angle and therefore is adjustable for any number of segments. Here the strip is cut, the strip flipped, and the other half of the segment included angle is cut in the same manner as the traditional sled above. However, it will need to be calibrated for each setting before accurate rings can be cut. This sled is the one most frequently used in open segment work since the cut angle accuracy is less critical. Because the segment falls from the edge of the sled, a zero clearance insert *(Photo 5)* is needed as well as a segment stop to set the cut off lengths. *(Photo 6)* Many commercial miter sleds with long protractor arms are reasonably accurate but may still require adjustments.

Its main features are:
- Commercially available
- Allows for cutting multiple angles
- Using a segment stop, it can cut segments very quickly
- Needed for open segment work

Zero clearance insert

5

Segment stop

The Chop Saw

While the chop saw operates similarly to the miter sled, it requires modifications to cut small pieces safely and repeatedly. A back fence (zero clearance fence) and stop assembly must be constructed. A safety hold down is also needed to keep fingers clear of the cutting area and secure the wood during the cut.

Like the miter fence the chop saw requires calibration of the angle for each cut angle. While many high end saws do have adjustable stops, their angle setting must still be checked and perhaps recalibrated. For open segment work the indicated angles and stops will be sufficiently accurate. A small adjustment of the angle can be made by adding a shim behind the zero clearance fence. Once the angle is set and calibrated it should not be readjusted until the project cutting is completed.

Its main features are:
- May already be in your shop not requiring the purchase of an additional piece of bulky equipment
- Segments can be stacked and gang cut speeding up production

The Chop Saw

The Wedgie Sled

30-60-90 triangle
setting up a
Wedgie Sled

The Wedgie Sled™

The Wedgie Sled, developed by wood artist, Jerry Bennett, is designed specifically for ring segmented construction and eliminates most of the setup errors of the saw or sled. Two parallel fences are set to the included segment angle then one edge of the segment is cut against the first fence and the second edge is cut against the second fence creating the desired included angle. The strip is not flipped as it is cut. Setup only requires a wedge with the desired included angle such as a 30-60-90 triangle *(Photo 9)* for 12 segment rings or purchased angle plates

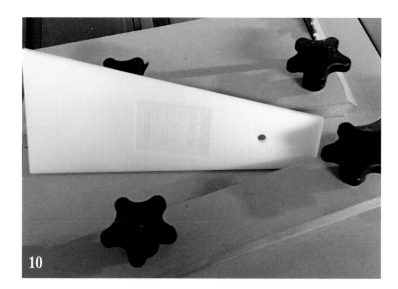

Wedgie Sled with
a plate for setting
24 segment

Full Wedgie Sled set
up with all pieces
in place

for other segment rings. *(Photo 10)* This wedge is the source of the sled's accuracy and repeatability.

A zero clearance insert and a segment stop are required. Check the appendix for more information on their construction. *(Photo 11)*

Its main features are:

- Eliminates most setup errors and cutting inaccuracies
- With precision wedges it can be quickly reset for many cutting angles
- Overcomes errors in the table saw setup
- Simple to construct

De-burring
a segment

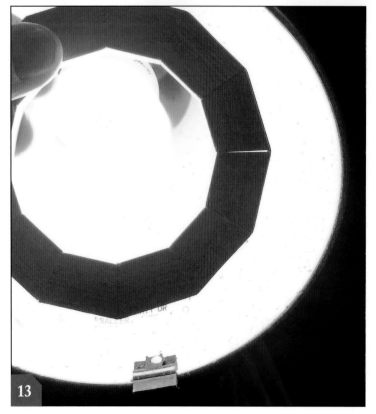

Checking for gaps with a bright light

Cutting Segments and Fitting Rings

Once the segments are cut and sorted, they require cleanup of any burrs remaining from the cutting process. Sand carefully to remove the burrs while not sanding the cut faces *(Photo 12)*. Test the ring's fit by using a rubber band and a bright back light. *(Photo 13)* If no light is visible through the ring glue it! If small errors occur use the half-ring method to correct them. If larger fitting errors appear, there is an error in the saw or sled being used.

Half-Ring Method

The half-ring method is used to correct small errors in cutting by gluing the ring into halves, placing a pivot between the two halves and clamping until the glue dries. If the pivot is centered carefully the angle errors will be accumulated at the pivot locations which can be sanded to dead flat.

The half-ring method

Checking sanding of a half ring

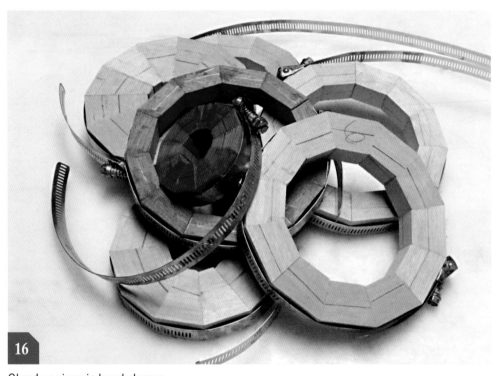

Glued up rings in band clamps

Mark the cut faces before sanding to allow checking for sanding flatness. A partially sanded line indicates that the face is not as yet totally flat. *(Photo 15)* Once the half-rings are flat, the two halves can be glued together to form a perfect ring.

Gluing Up a Ring

Use a flat pre-waxed surface for the gluing. You may prefer to use band clamps to secure the rings while the PVA wood glue dries. *(Photo 16)* Clamps from the same manufacturer can be ganged together to make larger rings.

3

Building a Hollow Vessel— The Complete Process

Prepare the Drawing and Cut List

As with the bowl in chapter one, it is important to create a full-scale drawing on graph paper and then add the stock thickness desired for each ring level. *(Figure 1)* Measure the inside and outside radii and subtract one from the other to determine the width of the stock needed for each ring. *(Figure 2)* Complete the cut list by adding the maximum length of stock required, calculate the segment

A ring segmented vessel

1

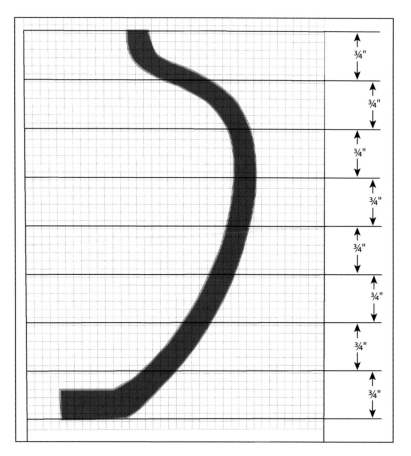

Figure 1

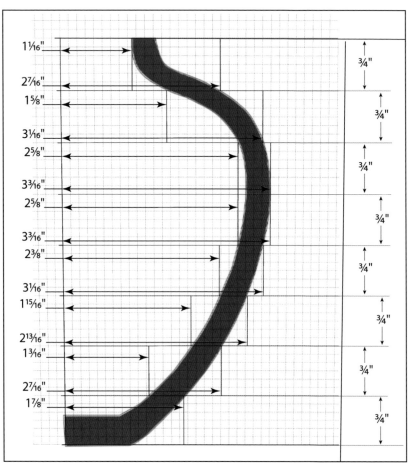

Figure 2

edge length from the circumference divided by the number of segments planned. *(See Cut List)*

Prepare the Components

Prepare the rings as in the bowl. Check the diameters to be sure there were no errors in cutting. *(Figure 3)* Assemble the ring onto two faceplate/glue assemblies building the bottom portion to the largest diameter; the top portion of the vessel will be built on the second faceplate/ glue block assembly. *(Figure 4)*

Turn the Vessel

After flattening the top ring of each assembly on the lathe, clamp the two halves together and turn the exterior shape following your drawing. *(Figure 5)*

The two sections then can be separated, hollowed individually and glued back together completing the hollow form.

Hollow Vessel Cut List

Row No.	Type	Material	Stock Thickness	Stock Width	Stock Length [1]	Segment Edge Length
8	12-seg. ring	Bloodwood	¾"	1⅜"	20"	1¼"
7	12-seg. ring	Yellow heart	¾"	1⁷⁄₁₆"	24"	1⅝"
6	12-seg. ring	Yellow heart	¾"	⁹⁄₁₆"	23"	1¹¹⁄₁₆"
5	12-seg. ring	Bloodwood	¾"	⁹⁄₁₆"	24½"	1¹¹⁄₁₆"
4	12-seg. ring	Yellow heart	¾"	¾"	24"	1⅝"
3	12-seg. ring	Yellow heart	¾"	⅞"	22½"	1½"
2	12-seg. ring	Yellow heart	¾"	1³⁄₁₆"	20½"	1⁵⁄₁₆"
1	Flat	Bloodwood	¾"	3¾"	3¾"	3¾"

1. Stock length includes allowance for ⅛" saw kerf and additional "safety" length.

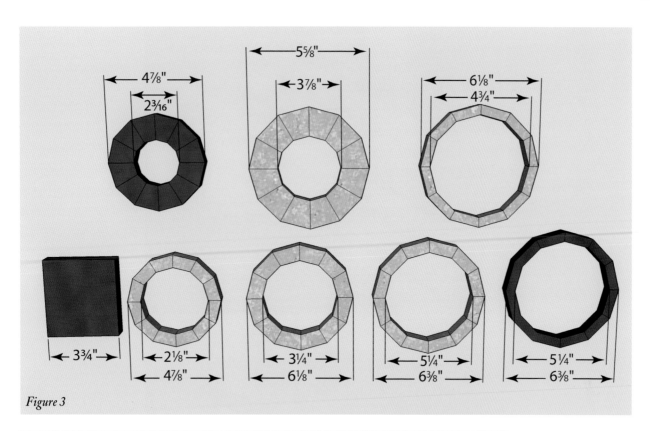

Figure 3

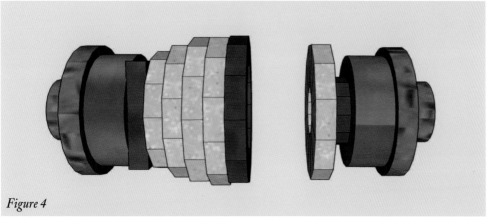

Figure 4

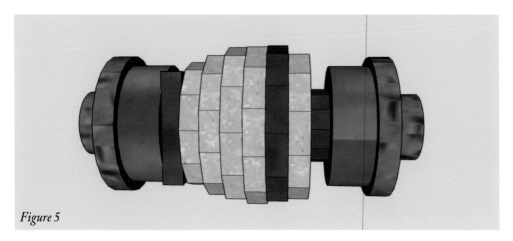

Figure 5

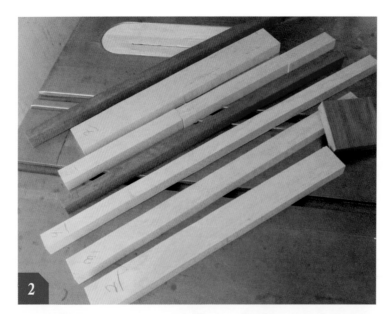

Strips cut to length and width

Cutting segments on the Wedgie sled

Bag the segments by ring number

Building the Project Vessel

Cut the strips to the width and lengths needed from the cut list, numbering each strip. *(Photo 2)*

In this project the segments are cut using the Wedgie Sled™ and a zero clearance insert with a "segment deflector" attached which keeps the segments away from the spinning saw blade. *(Photo 3)*

Bag the segments separately by ring number. *(Photo 4)* Using 220 grit sandpaper, deburr the segments carefully.

Build the Rings

Glue up each ring using band clamps or rubber bands. If the rings don't fit well use the half ring method to complete them.

Stack the rings in order to check the correctness of your planning and cutting. *(Photo 5)*

Number the edge of each ring in preparation for sanding the faces. *(Photo 6)*

Rings stacked in order

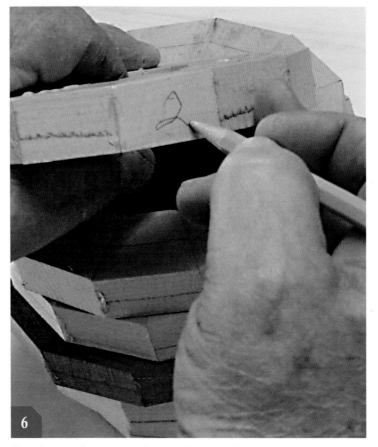

Transferring the ring numbers to the ring edge

7

Preparing the first glue block by flattening

8

Sanding after flattening

Build the Project on Two Faceplate/Glue Block Assemblies

Assemble and flatten two faceplate and glue block assemblies. Check the flatness with a straight edge. *(Photo 7)*

After the assemblies are as flat as you can achieve with turning tools, use a sanding stick with 80 grit sandpaper attached to complete the flattening process. *(Photo 8)*

Build the Vessel

Start the assembly by flattening one side of the top ring on a sanding disk or disc sander. *(Photo 9)*

The top ring is centered on one of the glue block assemblies; here we are using a live center cone assembly as an alignment aid. *(Photo 10)*

Prepare all other rings by sanding one side flat on a disc or processing through a thickness sander that will sand both sides flat and parallel. *(Photo 11)*

Flattening the top ring on a sanding disk

Gluing on the top ring with a Oneway alignment cone

Thickness sanding the rings to parallel faces

Trimming the base corners

Gluing on the base

Flattening ring seven with a gouge

Prepare the vessel base by trimming its corners on a bandsaw to save turning difficulties later. *(Photo 12)*

Flatten the base and glue it onto the other glue block assembly. *(Photo 13)*

After each level is added it must be checked for flatness. If the ring appears out of alignment with the lathe axis use your gouge to bring it back into alignment. *(Photo 14)*

Once the alignment error is corrected the ring should be sanded with the sanding stick before the next ring is attached.

When adding a ring, mark the center of one segment and align that mark with a glue joint of the preceding ring to assure correct "brick-laid" configuration. *(Photo 15)*

Build the base section only up to the widest ring in the planned vessel. *(Photo 16)*

When the two assemblies have been completed, re-flatten the top ring of each on the lathe so that when clamped together they run properly in line. When this is done you are ready for turning. *(Photo 17)*

Aligning ring six

Building to the
widest ring

Both assemblies
flattened and ready
to turn

Top-bottom clamped on the lathe and ready to turn

18

19

Exterior turned

20

Interior of the base hollowed

Turn the Vessel

Clamp the two assemblies together on the lathe. A live center with lathe threads will allow the top assembly to remain rigidly in place on the tailstock. *(Photo 18)*

Turn the exterior to match the drawing leaving the base oversized for support during the next steps. *(Photo 19)*

Remove the top assembly and hollow out the interior of the base section working from the top ring downward in steps. You may need a round nosed scraper to finish the deepest portion of the base. *(Photo 20)*

When the hollowing is completed, sand and seal the interior. *(Photo 21)*

Replace the base with the top section and hollow it out. *(Photo 22)*

With your calipers check the wall thickness of the base section and match the wall thickness of the top ring of the base assembly; then seal the top's interior. *(Photo 23)*

Sealing the interior of the base assembly

Top interior hollowed

Wall thickness matched at the glue line

24

Preparing to glue on the top section

Close the Vessel and Complete

Remount the base assembly on the headstock. Add a thin bead of glue to the top assembly. *(Photo 24)*

Using the lathe as an alignment tool, glue the two assemblies together assuring glue squeeze out and segment alignment. Do not wipe away the excess glue. *(Photo 25)*

Part off the top's neck ring from the glue block when the glue is dry. *(Photo 26)*

Clean up the neck exterior and interior carefully. *(Photo 27)*

Clean up the vessel exterior removing excess glue and sanding. *(Photo 28)*

Reduce the base to its final dimension and add a small parting cut at its bottom to ease sanding. *(Photo 29)* Complete sanding and apply a topcoat. *(Photo 30)*

Part off and complete the bottom of the base. *(Photo 31)*

25

Vessel glued together

26

Neck section
parted off

Neck section shaped interior and exterior

Rough sanding of the exterior

Base reduced and shaped

Top coat applied

The finished
hollow vessel

4 Simple Design Enhancements

This chapter deals with simple actions that can advance or improve the appearance of your project.

Splitting a Ring

Sometimes the design calls for thin rings that would be difficult to make; therefore making thicker rings and splitting them into thinner sections is easier and safer.

Splitting a ring on the lathe

1

Thicker rings can be glued onto the project, turned round, then split using a thin parting tool. Be sure to make light, overlapping cuts. *(Photo 1)*

Rings can be split on the bandsaw using a tall, resaw fence and a push block with a course abrasive mounted to its face in order to prevent slippage during the cut. Bandsaw cuts must be done slowly and with lateral pressure toward the resaw fence as the downward cutting pressure of the bandsaw blade will try to rotate the ring into the blade during the entry and exit portion of the cut. *(Photo 2)*

Mixing Colors and Rotation

Changing the amount of rotation between the rings can enhance a simple brick-laid vessel. Use a percentage of the segment edge length of each ring being added. Alternating colors within the rings can also enhance the effect. *(Photo 3)*

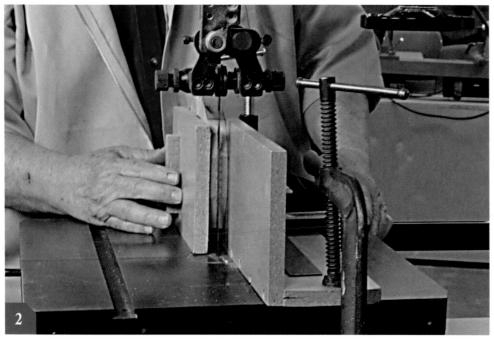

Splitting a ring on the band saw

Spiral brick laid vessel

4

Using spacers

Adding Spacers

Spacers create the appearance of additional, smaller segments without the need to cut angles. The spacer is cut square (remember to maintain horizontal grain alignment) and its width is subtracted from the planned segment edge length. It maintains the desired ring diameter and adds additional contrast without additional angles cut. *(Photo 4)*

5

Vessel with/without veneers

6

Painted vessel

Using Veneers

Using veneers enhances the design by creating crisp lines between abutting colors. *(Photo 5)*

Veneer can be found in all colors as well as wood species. They require some special handling during cutting, as they are fragile and subject to easy tears. Use a very sharp utility knife and a hard cutting surface. Since they are generally made from dyed, porous woods, they adsorb the moisture from the wood glue and expand and distort if not tightly clamped until the glue is totally dry—several hours.

7

Dyed bracelet

Paint & Dyes

Paint and dyes can add to a simple construction made with inexpensive timber. Consider milk paint, acrylics, and aniline dyes to add color and interest. *(Photos 6 and 7)*

8

Acrylic vessel

Alternative Materials

If you can cut it, sand it and glue it, you can segment it! Consider alternative materials such as plastics, acrylics, Corian™ or other non-woods. *(Photo 8)*

The Floating Foot

A vessel containing a solid foot greater that 4 inches in diameter may be subject to failure due to cross grain stresses between the solid foot and the lower rings. Also vessels built with a pie-shaped base will be subject to stresses due to wood movement. *(Photo 9)*

The solution to these problems is a "floating foot" which allows the solid foot to move separately from the segmented vessel. *(Photo 10)*

The floating foot can also be used as an esthetic enhancement.

Acacia bowl with a cracked foot

A floating foot

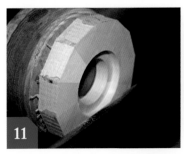

Step ne: mortise the base ring

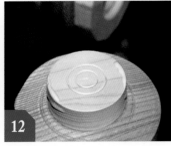

Step two: prepare a floating foot insert

Step three: flatten the insert after gluing in

Step four: add ring two to cover the insert

Here are the steps:
Mount the first ring of the vessel on the glue block assembly and cut a square groove ½–⅓ of its ring's thickness. This ring will become the visible base of the vessel. *(Photo 11)* Separately create an insert disc slightly smaller in diameter than the groove. Add glue to the end grain only. *(Photo 12)*

After the insert is glued in, flatten it to the level of the first ring. *(Photo 13)*

Cover the insert with the second ring, which will have been made with a smaller ID than that of the inserted disk in order to cover the glue joint. Then continue to build the vessel. *(Photo 14)*

Advanced Cutting on the Wedgie Sled™
Angled/Leaning Rings

Segmented rings can be cut with a tilted saw blade creating interesting spiral designs. Cutting segments on the Wedgie Sled with a blade leaning will produce right leaning segments from the first fence and left leaning segments from the other fence. You will need to cut twice as many segments as expected for a leaning ring—however the yield will be two rings: one left leaning and one right leaning. Spacers can also be cut at the same angle emphasizing the ring's lean. *(Photo 15)*

Slanted ring with spacers

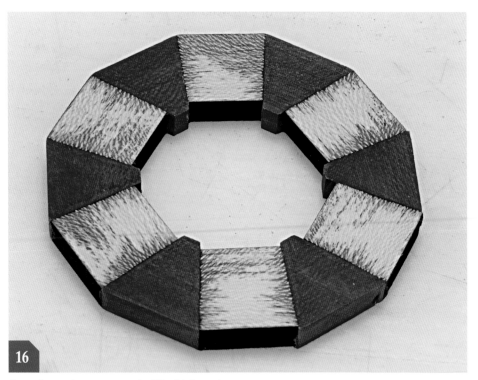

Complementary segments fitted into a ring

Complementary Segments

While the included angle between the two fences produces perfect rings when following the directions given in chapter 2, the angle between each individual fence and the saw blade may differ. Segments cut only on one fence will have a different angle from segments cut only on the other fence. *However* those segments when put together will still add up to a ring. The cut angles will create complementary segments as in this picture. *(Photo 16)*

The two actions can be combined into a leaning ring with segments cut at complementary angles. *(Photo 17)*

Slanted complementary segments fitted into a ring

5 Techniques for Making Feature Rings

This chapter presents several techniques that can be used to create your own designs. Cutting and shaping components utilizing your woodworking tools is complicated by the additional need to maintain grain alignment wherever possible.

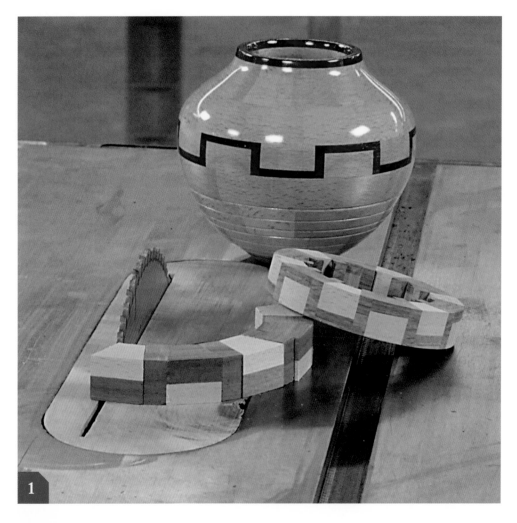

The Greek key design

1

Cutting spacers and laminates

Laying out the Greek key ring

Laminations and Spacers— the Greek Key Design

This pattern *(Photo 1)* utilizes laminations and spacers to create the design. Variations of this can add simple interest points to your next vessel.

Laminate two wood species to equal the desired ring thickness. Then cut spacers for the darker species with a length equal to its lamination thickness. It is important to maintain the longitudinal grain alignment for the spacers. *(Photo 2)*

Subtract the spacer thickness from the planned segment edge length and cut the segments from the lamination.

Flip every other segment, insert the spacers and glue up the ring. *(Photo 3)*

Thunderbird design

Miter cutting two colors at 45 degrees

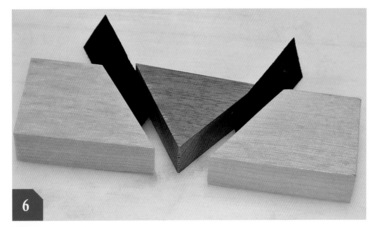

Flip and insert veneers

Glue and clamp

Cutting Slices to Create a Pattern— the Thunderbird Design

Miter cut two dissimilar colors of wood at the same angle—try 45 degrees first. The darker species should be cut to a point and will be the Thunderbird. *(Photo 5)*

Flip the lighter species, insert the darker species and strips of veneer between. *(Photo 6)*

Glue up the assembly clamping carefully to secure tight joints. *(Photo 7)*

Clean up all glue and assure that the assembly is square.

On your table saw slice the assembly into ⅛" to ³⁄₁₆" wide strips. *(Photo 8)* **Safe cutting technique is important to prevent kickbacks and protect fingers. Always use a push stick.**

Flip the strips and reassemble into the "T" Bird pattern. Try different arrangements until you are satisfied. You may choose to leave out one or two strips to improve the design. *(Photo 9)*

Square the stock and slice into strips

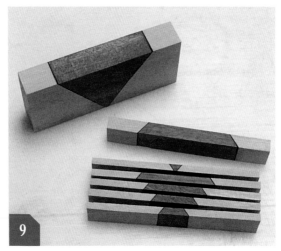

Flip and restack the strips

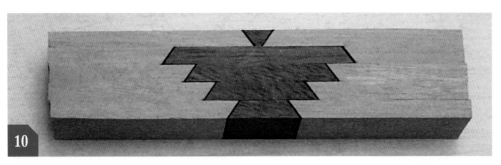

Glue the strips together

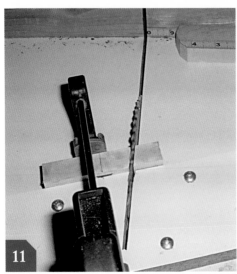

(ABOVE LEFT) Mark the center and cut the segment angles from each side

(ABOVE) Experiment

Glue the assembly into the "T" Bird design clamping very carefully to keep all components in alignment. *(Photo 10)*

To cut the segments mark the center of each assembly to assure that the pattern is centered in the final segment and cut the angle carefully from each side. *(Photo 11)*

Assemble the segments into the desired ring.

Try experimenting with different thicknesses and different arrangements to create other possible patterns. *(Photo 12)*

13

Zig-Zag vessel

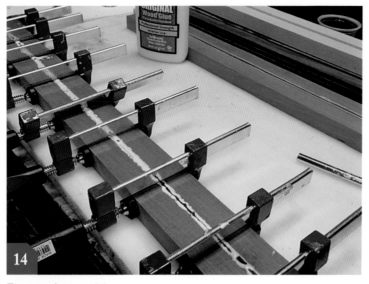

14

Zig-zag glue up strip

Cutting With Precision and Accuracy—the Zig-Zag

The purpose of this design *(Photo 13)* is to develop very precise cutting and assembly techniques necessary to build a ring with sharp, aligned points. Segments must come together inside and outside equally so that turning will not reveal misalignments.

Planning the Zig-Zag Pattern

Build a laminate with a contrasting color band in the center. In the beginning maintain a wide field band on each side to account for eventual trimming. *(Photo 14)*

From your vessel plan determine the segment height and edge length desired and transfer this information to a piece of graph paper. *(Photo 15)*

Cut a window in the paper exactly ½ of the segment width desired. *(Photo 16)*

Place this template over the laminate strip and locate the most desirable position. The color band should intersect both sides of the window at the same distance from the top and bottom and not pass out the top or bottom edges. *(Photo 17)*

Trace a line on the wood parallel to the edge of the graph paper. *(Photo 18)*

With a protractor measure the angle of the line; this will be the angle at which you cut the laminate. *(Photo 19)*

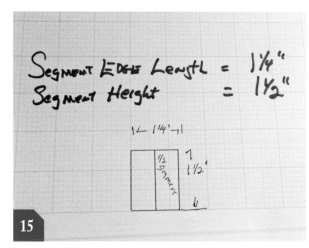

15

Making a drawing of the planned segment

16

Cutting out a half segment window

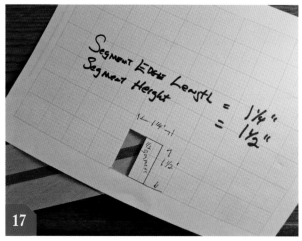

17

Place window over the laminate and find the best position

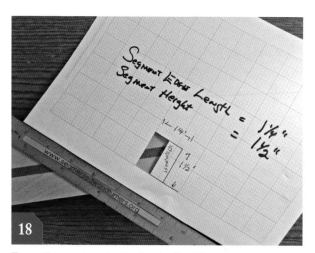

18

Trace the angle onto the laminate strip

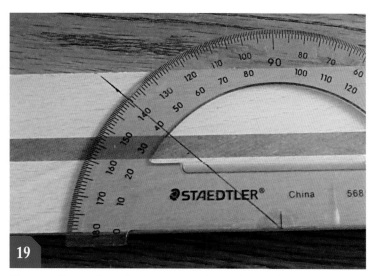

19

Measure the angle and set your miter fence to match

20

Cut the laminate into half segment strips

Cut the Segment Components

Cut the strip at the measured angle and into strips ½ segment wide; two strips will make up a segment. Save the square cut off at the ends of the strip for use later. *(Photo 20)*

After cleaning off any burrs, flip every other slice and assemble all the strips into a tray and secure with double-sided tape and the end cut offs. *(Photo 21)*

At your table saw trim one edge square. Flip the strips end for end in the tray and trim the opposite edge. *(Photo 22)*

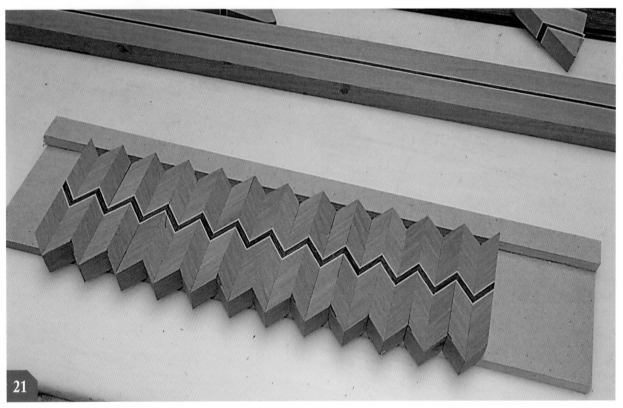

21

Ready to trim the first edge square

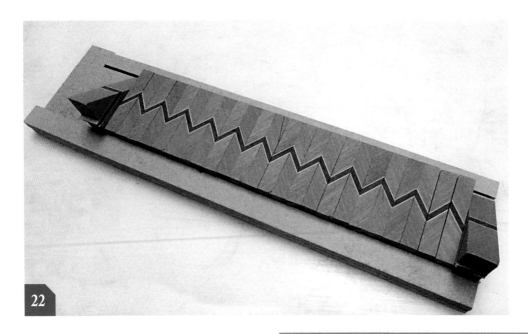

Flip and
trim the
second edge

22

Completing the Segments

Assemble and glue the pairs into segment blanks flipping every other strip and carefully aligning the points. *(Photo 23)*

At your table saw set the fence system to allow you to cut one half of the segment by measuring from the center of the design. Flip the segment and cut the other side of the segment.

23

Glue into pairs first

Building the Ring

While it may be easy to glue up the full ring and get perfect alignment most beginners should assemble pairs of segments, then pairs of pairs until the half ring is completed. Then the two half rings can be carefully assembled. This technique will allow you to focus on the perfect alignment of the segment points inside and outside the design. *(Photo 24)*

Build pairs
into a ring

24

Simple diamonds

25

Sander with a
90-degree fence

26

Using a Disc Sander with a Sanding Stop— Simple Diamonds

The purpose of the next design *(Photo 25)* is to introduce the use of the disc sander as a sizing tool. It will require building a 90-degree fence system with an adjustable segment sanding stop such as the one pictured. The sander also should be checked for square of the table to the sanding disk. This system will be very valuable to you for many future designs. *(Figure 26)*

Here is an overview of the process:

- Cut four light colored field pieces per diamond *(Figure 27)*
- Cut two dark triangles per diamond *(Figure 28)*
- Sand off the points on all field pieces *(Figure 29)*

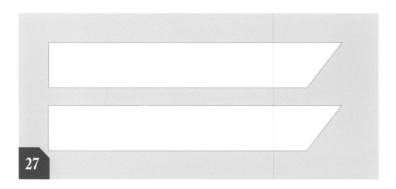

27 Cut four light colored strips

28 Cut dark strip and flip to cut a triangle

29 Sand the tips of the light strip

DESIGN OF SANDING FENCE SYSTEM

For the next two techniques, and other precision processes using your disc sander, you will need to build a fence system similar to the one pictured. Important features are:

- The sanding sled rides smoothly in your sander's miter slot
- The sled contains a permanent fence constructed 90 degrees to the sanding disc face
- A hold down clamp is required for the adjustable sanding stop to set specific dimensions
- The face of the adjustable sanding stop is parallel with the sander's face

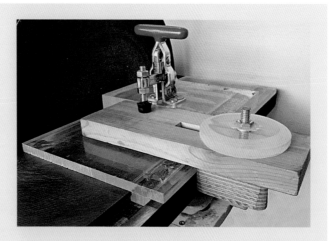

Mine is built to fit my model sander. It is 13" wide and 6½" deep and is built from ³/₁₆" acrylic material which does not change dimensions over time.

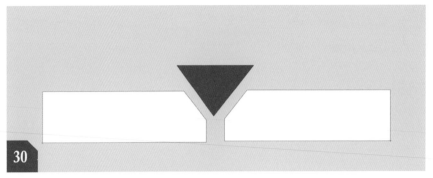

30

Glue in a triangle between two light strips

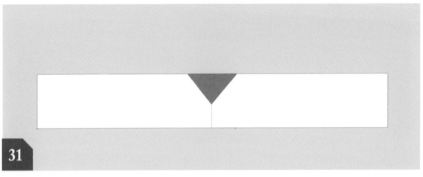

31

Sand flat

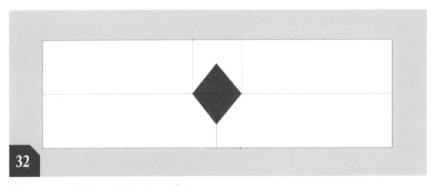

32

Reverse one strip and glue together

- Glue two field pieces together and insert a dark triangle piece *(Figure 30)*
- Clean up surface *(Figure 31)*
- Glue two assemblies together to form the diamond *(Figure 32)*

Prepare the Components
Mill Wood

Mill two wood species to the same width and thickness. One dark for the diamonds and one lighter for the field surrounding the diamond. The dimensions will be one half the segment ring height and equal to the planned wall thickness. The length of the field pieces is not critical as they will eventually be recut into the segments; but they must exceed one half the planned segment edge length.

Cut Components

On the light colored field pieces, cut an angle of 15–45 degrees; an angle of 15 degrees will give a narrow diamond while a more obtuse angle will make fatter diamonds. Cut the opposite end square and to a fixed, predetermined length. They will be recut later. You will need four field pieces for each diamond. *(Photo 33)*

Cut the dark wood components to the same angle; flip the piece over and cut it again to create a triangle with a sharp point. Several trial cuts may be necessary to set the miter stop to get the sharp point needed. The cutting angle must be the same as with the field pieces. You will need two triangles for each diamond. *(Photo 34)*

Sand Off Field Piece Points

Using your disc sander with a sanding stop installed, sand the angled face of the field pieces to create a flat about ¼ to ⅓ of the height of the piece. All pieces must be sanded to the same length; therefore, set the stop on the fence to prevent over sanding *(Photo 35)*

Field pieces cut

Diamond pieces cut

Sanding a flat on the field pieces

36

Components ready
to assemble

Pressing into the V

37

38

Sanding flat and square

After all the components
are cut and sanded, deburr
all pieces. *(Photo 36)*

Build Half Diamonds

On a flat surface and against a
straight edge glue two field pieces
together at the sanded faces and
press one diamond component
into the "V." The glue will "tack"
in a few seconds and the assembly
can be moved. *(Photo 37)*

Sand the faces of the half
diamond assemblies flat and parallel
removing any protruding portion
of the inserted dark triangle. Again
use your custom sanding fence
system and the stop at the disc
sander to assure that all sanded
components are identical. *(Photo 38)*

Complete the Diamond

Assemble the two halves
carefully aligning the dark
triangles. *(Photo 39)*

Cut the segments by marking
the center of the assembly and
cutting the segment angle
from each edge. *(Photo 40)*

39

Assembling the two halves

40

Cutting the segment angles

Precision Diamonds Using the Disk Sander and Custom Angled Fence

Making this style of sanded diamonds requires the construction of an additional fence matching the exact angle required for the diamonds. This is necessary to build the project.

Here are the steps in the process:

- Plan your project. The field pieces and the dark diamond center pieces can be cut the same dimensions; however, you may choose to cut the field pieces longer to allow more space between the diamonds in your feature ring. A drawing based of the feature ring diameter, height and ring thickness is important in the planning.

In this project a custom, movable, sanding stop will be created replacing the square, 90-degree one used in the previous project. Once the fence is created to match the desired angle, it will be used to produce the exact angle on all the field pieces. As the field pieces are constructed into a diamond the same sanding stop will be used to prepare each face prior to adding the next component. Here is what the custom sanding stop looks like for one project.

Cut four light and one dark rectangles

Mark the center of one dark and sand to the line

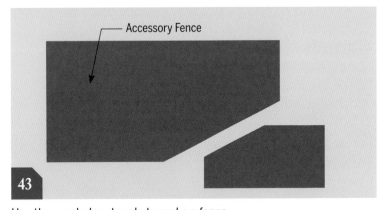

Accessory Fence

Use the sanded rectangle to make a fence

Sand the one corner of all the pieces

- Cut four light colored field pieces and one dark center piece for each diamond. *(Figure 41)*
- Mark the center of the top and one edge on one dark center piece and sand to split the line. *(Figure 42)*
- Using your disc sander make a movable sanding stop to match the sanded angle just created. *(Figure 43)*
- Use the new movable sanding stop to sand a corner of a light colored field piece to the same angle; the trial piece should be sanded to remove approximately 60% of its height. Reset the movable sanding stop and lock it at that dimension. Sand all remaining light colored field pieces using the stop to set the sanded edge length. *(Figure 44)*
- Glue one light colored piece to the sanded corner of the dark piece overlapping the piece's sanded edges on both sides *(Figure 45)*
- Use the moveable sanding stop to sand the opposite top edge of the dark center piece stopping at the intersection of at the top edge and recently added light colored field piece. *(Figure 46)*
- Glue on a second light colored field piece to the just sanded edge again overlapping at top and bottom. *(Figure 47)*
- Using the square original parallel fence, flatten the top of the assembly. *(Figure 48)*

Glue one of the field pieces to a sanded dark corner

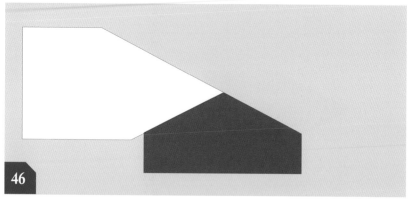

Sand the second corner

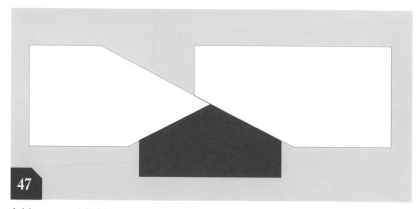

Add a second field piece

Sand the top flat and flip

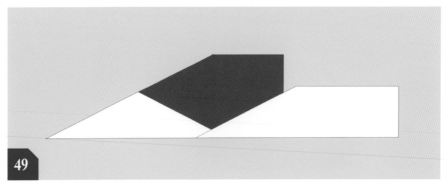

Sand the third corner

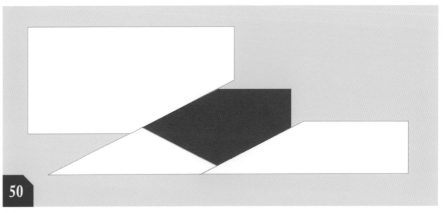

Add the third field piece

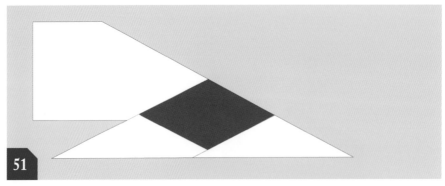

Sand the fourth corner

- Flip the assembly over and sand a third corner as was done on the opposite side. *(Figure 49)*
- Add a third light colored field piece overlapping the intersections as before. *(Figure 50)*
- Finally sand the last corner. *(Figure 51)*
- Add the fourth light colored field piece. *(Figure 52)*
- Sand the just completed edge flat and parallel to the opposite edge. *(Figure 53)*
- Mark out the segment edge length from the center of the diamond pattern and cut the required segment angles. *(Figure 54)*

52

Add the last field piece

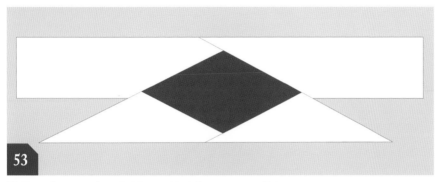

53

Flatten the completed sides so that they are parallel

54

Mark the segment edge length from the center

55

Mark out the
diamond centers

(RIGHT) Free-hand
sand to the line

(BELOW) Making
the fence from
the sanded
diamond master

56

57

- After all components are cut, the
diamond center piece master is
marked by connecting the center
of the top edge to the center of
one end. This defines the angle
included in the diamond to be.
(Photo 55)
- Using your disc sander, free-
hand sand the marked corner
to split the line. *(Photo 56)*
Place the sanded angle (the
split line) against your 90-degree
fence on the disc sander and use

Sand all field pieces and one corner of the diamonds to the fence angle

All steps in sanding and gluing the diamond

it to create a custom sanding stop with a matching angle. This sanding stop will be used in place of the 90-degree fence for all remaining sanded angles. *(Photo 57)*

All the field pieces are now sanded using the new fence to the same exact angle. One corner of the dark center pieces is also sanded to the same angle. When sanding the dark center piece reset the sanding stop to sand the dark pieces to match the original marked one. *(Photo 58)*

The diamond is assembled by adding one field piece to the sanded diamond corner, sanding the next corner to the same angle removing waste material then adding another field piece, until all four corners are completed. *(Photo 59)*

6 Setting Up and Building an Open Segment Vessel

Open segment construction is both easy and more tedious at the same time.

It is simpler since the segments do not need to be cut as precisely because they do not touch each other. *(Photo 1)*

It is more tedious because segments are placed individually in order to create the gaps needed.

Open segment cut angle

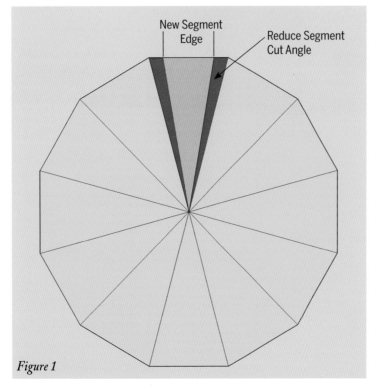

New Segment Edge

Reduce Segment Cut Angle

Figure 1

Calculations

For an open segment vessel, the segment's included angle is reduced by a fixed percentage and the segment edge length is also decreased by the same percentage. *(Figure 1)*

As an example, if you desire a 25% gap between segments and the initial ring-segment plan called for a 1-inch segment with a 30 degree included angle, the results would be ¾" segments with an included angle of 22.5 degrees.

Cutting Segments

A custom sled with adjustable angles and a positive stop can be built to accommodate the angles required for your projects. *(Photo 2)* Also a commercial adjustable miter sled used with a segment stop will allow for any angle. *(Photo 3)* Either type of system will provide adequate cutting accuracy since the segments do not touch.

1 Open segment vessel

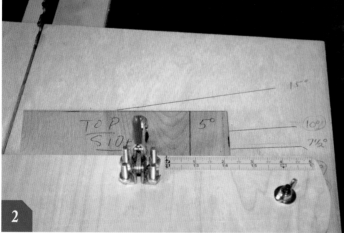

2

3

Indexing

Construction requires two fixtures: one indexing assembly needed to rotate the project a set number of degrees for placing the segments, and one to assist in gluing the segments at the correct radial distance and in the center of the project.

Commercial Indexing plates can be purchased from sources listed in the appendix. These plates contain rows of indexing holes allowing you to set the rotation between segments for many different projects. A pin will be inserted into the appropriate hole

(ABOVE LEFT)
Cutting sled and stop

(ABOVE)
A commercial miter sled

Commercial indexing plates

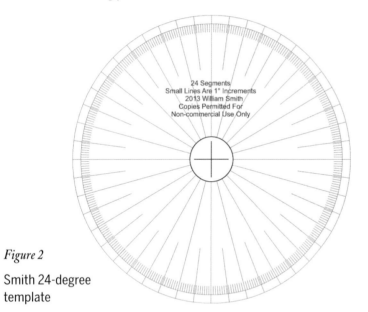

Figure 2

Smith 24-degree template

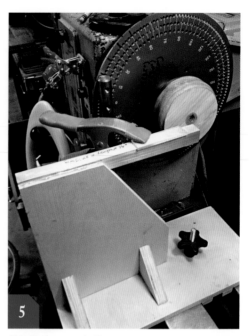

JLR fixture on lathe

to lock the project in place while the segment is glued in. *(Photo 4)*

Custom plates can also be constructed from printed radial drawings attached to your own disk. A pointer and arresting mechanism would be created to mark and lock the correct location. Check the appendix for the source of radial drawings created by Bill Smith specifically for the segmented turning community. *(Figure 2)*

Indexing plates should contain twice the number of divisions required for the project in order to allow accurate offset for the following row necessary to create the "brick laid" pattern.

Assembly Fixtures

Assembly fixtures assist the segmenter in placing each segment accurately at the correct distance for the center of that "ring" and at the rotational angle set by the indexing plate.

On the Lathe Fixture

The fixture for building an open segment vessel on the lathe must hold the segments at the center of the lathe's rotational axis and allow for measuring the radial distance from the center of rotation to the outside edge of the segment. (This is the radius of the ring being built) *(Photo 5)*

The assembly fixture for use on the lathe should align between the ways of the lathe with a locking

Added stop and
measuring tape
on fixture

hold that will keep the fixture
square to the project's face. A
hardware store aluminum angle
can be used to make the extension
arm which is constructed at the
lathe's center height and extends
to the center of rotation.

A "stick on tape" for measuring
the radii and a stop to set the
segment against are added. *(Photo 6)*

The commercial indexing wheel
was placed on the lathe spindle and
locked in place behind the faceplate.

Off the Lathe Fixture

Off the lathe assembly is done
vertically and requires the same
rotational indexing and segment
placement assemblies; with this
technique the two components
are assembled into a single
construction freeing the lathe
for other tasks. Gravity is now
an asset in holding segments in
place while the glue tacks.

This fixture *(Photo 7)* designed by
Jim Driskell uses a printed indexing
diagram placed below the project's
faceplate assembly. The segment

Driskell original fixture

placement arm is attached to a post
and can be raised and lowered as
the vessel is built up. The author's
fixture is similar in design. Here
the "T" track from a woodworking
dealer shows the adjustable segment
arm. A commercial indexing
plate is used with a locking pin
pressed into a matching hole
below the disk. *(Photo 8)*.

When building this style of
fixture, the vertical post is assembled
first and the segment placement arm
of angle aluminum is cut slightly

8

Authors' vertical open segment

9

Thread adapters

These thread adapters can be purchased or made from lathe thread/Morris taper adapters. A metal lathe will be required to reshape and shorten the taper shaft portion to fit into the hole drilled at the center of rotation. *(Photo 9)*

SegEasy™ Assembly Method

A third alternative technique, developed by Jerry Bennett, allows you to place a complete layer of segments at one time. Several versions are available for different segment counts. *(Photo 10)*

The segments must be cut with a 4-degree gap so that each segment will wedge into the fixture tightly. Rubber bands also help to hold the segments in place. SegEasy plates can be used for on or off lathe assembly.

Whether you choose to build your vessel on the lathe

longer than the radius of the indexing wheel being used. Drop the arm to the base and mark its exact end in order to locate the rotational thread fixture. This process assures that the thread fixture will be mounted at the exact center of rotation relative to the segment placement arm. Again a "stick on" ruler tape is helpful in setting the stop accurately.

In order to mount a faceplate/ glue block assembly on which to build your project, a lathe thread adapter is required that will allow rotation of the faceplate on which the project is being assembled.

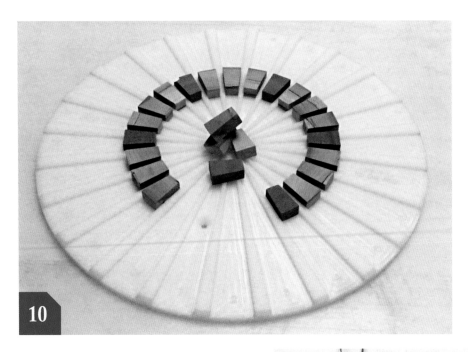

10

SegEasy plates

or off the lathe the process
will follow the same steps.

- Create a drawing and construct
  a table for dimensions as you did
  for your first segmented bowl.
- Add a column for the additional
  open segment dimensions that
  are required. The ring radius, the
  reduced segment edge length,
  and the new segment cut angle.
- Reduce the segment edge
  dimension by 20% (recommended
  for first vessels) and record this
  new segment edge length.
- Record the outside radius for
  each "ring". *(Photo 11)*
- Reduce the cut angle by 20% and
  record this as the new cut angle.

Cut the Segments

Segments will be cut in the same manner
as for earlier ring segmented projects.
However, the cut angle and segment
edge lengths will be from the table
created for this open segment project.
Be sure to clean up all burrs. *(Photo 12)*

Project name:

Ring number	Ring OD (inches)	Ring ID (inchs)	Ring Radius (OD)	Number of segments	Segment length (inches)	Segment width (inches)
1	4.625		2 5/16	1	-0	2 5/16
2	5.825	2.625	2 15/16	24	6/8	1 10/16
3					7/8	1 5/16
4					1	1 3/16
					1 1/8	1 1/16
					1 2/8	15/16
					1 2/8	12/16
					1 2/8	11/1

11

Determine the
ring's radius

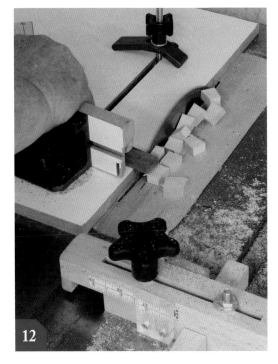

12

Cutting
segments
for an open
segment project

Setting up the indexing on the lathe

Adding the first segment

On the Lathe Assembly

Install the indexing plate behind the faceplate/glue block assembly which will lock it in place. Determine the indexing pattern and which holes to mark and use. For a 24-segment vessel use the 48-hole pattern to allow for accurate offset of the following row. *(Photo 13)*

Set up the segment placement fixture close to the faceplate. From your calculation sheet locate the radius of the first ring and set the fixture's stop. *(Photo 14)*

Add glue to the first segment and place it against the stop and press it onto the glue block/base assembly. Allow it to sit in place for a minimum of 20 seconds to allow the glue to tack.

Rotate the indexing plate to the next position and add the next segment. Be sure to wait for the glue to tack. For smaller segments and tight fits, a pair of tweezers may help. *(Photo 15)*

When the row is completed, allow additional drying time before sanding the completed level flat. A sanding stick placed flat against the completed row will assure that the next row added will sit flat and glue properly. *(Photo 16)*

Reset the indexing to a position that rotates the assembly one half a segment further creating the "brick laid" pattern.

Using tweezers to place a small segment

Sanding the first open segment ring

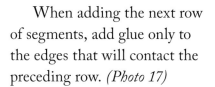

Use only a little glue

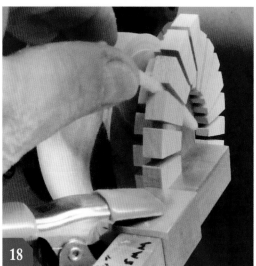

Use damp pipe cleaners to remove excess glue

When adding the next row of segments, add glue only to the edges that will contact the preceding row. *(Photo 17)*

As the assembly continues use a dampened pipe cleaner to remove glue squeeze out from between segments. *(Photo 18)*

An alternate indexing wheel

19

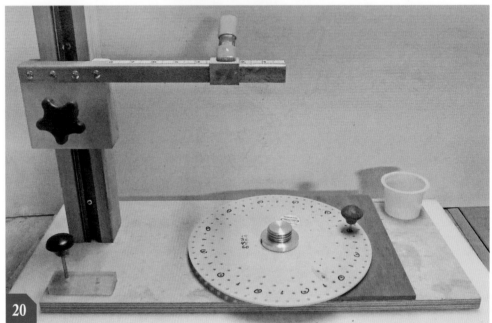

Vertical fixture ready to use

20

Off the Lathe Assembly

Using a vertical off-lathe fixture follows the same assembly steps. The face plate assembly is screwed to a thread adapter which in turn secures the indexing wheel horizontally. The hole pattern is selected. Here the correct holes are marked to reduce setting errors. *(Photo 19)*

The segment stop is clamped to the placement arm at the appropriate radius. *(Photo 20)*

The segment placement arm is lowered to the assembly and segments are added. Remember

21

Adding segments vertically

to use a small amount of glue
and clean up between segments
as you go. *(Photo 21)*

Using the SegEasy Plates for Assembly

The SegEasy plates allow for pre-positioning the segments at the proper spacing a full row at a time. The segments are wedged loosely into the slots of a plate. *(Photo 22)*

22

SegEasy plate with a full ring of segments ready to go

Attaching a row of segments with the SegEasy plate

23

Vessel ready to turn

24

assembled as was done with the ring segmented vessel earlier. When each component is completed, flatten its top-most ring to aid in the next steps. *(Photo 24)*

Clamp the top and bottom sections together in the lathe in order to turn the exterior shape. *(Photo 25)*

Before separating the sections and turning the interior, mark the exact alignment with tape so that the sections can be easily re-aligned for final gluing. *(Photo 26)*

Hollow each section separately; re-true the top edge if necessary before final assembly. It may be easier to add finish to the interior at this time. Place a small amount of glue on each segment and clamp them together on the lathe while aligning the tape. *(Photo 27)*

After the vessel halves are glued and clamped together, do

With a rubber band holding the segments in place for added security, the assembly is centered with the lathe tailstock, glue is added, and the rotational placement is achieved by eye. *(Photo 23)*

Turning the Vessel

For open segment vessels a top and bottom portion are separately

Clamped together
ready to turn
the exterior

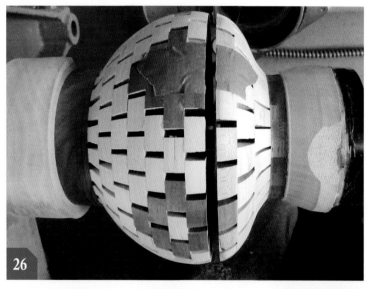

Marking
for realignment

Preparing to glue
the vessel together

Allow squeezed
out glue to dry

28

not wipe away the squeezed out
glue; allow it to dry and cut it
away later to protect the wood for
the finishing process. *(Photo 28)*

When the glue is dry the
exterior can be cleaned up. Finish
is added to the exterior, interior
and with a small pipe cleaner,
between the segments. *(Photo 29)*

29

Completed and
finished vessel

Bowl from a Board

7

Bowl from a Board is a process of laminating wood, re-sawing, cutting out rings, and assembling to create designs that appear both interesting and confusing to the non-trained viewer. Thus the process's other name: Dizzy Bowls. The most important step is in creating the cut plan that will yield the desired vessel.

The technique presented here is a multi-board technique that reduces the projects' difficulty, increases the ring overlap and thus the wall thickness, and is simpler to cut and prepare. From the drawing,

1

Bowl from a Board

boards will be prepared, rings cut, stacked, and the vessel turned.

The shape of the planned vessel dictates the amount of ring overlap and therefore the number of laminated boards required.

Prepare Your Plan

Bowls from a board projects are more interesting when the layers in the project are relatively thin. For first projects create a drawing with a slope of approximately 45 degrees and a smooth flowing curve. This design will allow rings to be cut cleanly from two boards for the glue up as shown in the illustration. *(Figure 2)* Bowls or vessels that have compound curves or more vertical edges will require more boards to be prepared in order to cut all the rings needed for the desired overlap. *(Figure 3)*

Draw your plan on graph paper, add the dimensions of the layers you desire, marking their inner and outer radii. Decide on the number of laminates required by determining how each ring can be cut from one or more boards without overlapping,

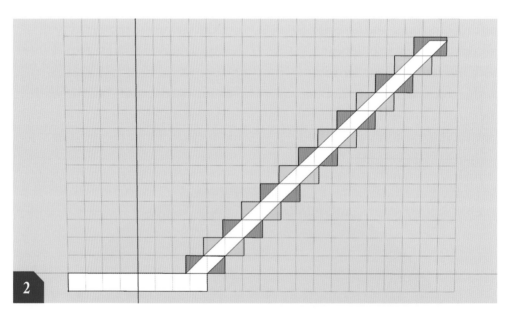

Drawing with a 45-degree lamination

2

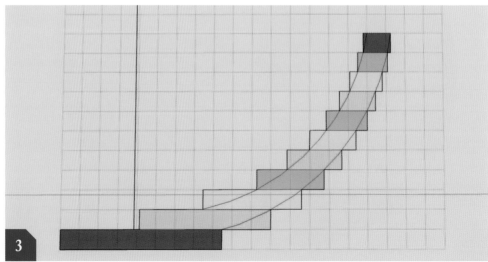

A more complex BFB requiring four laminations

3

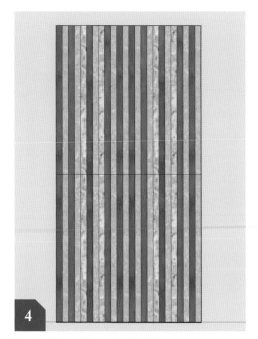

4

Lamination strip cut in half

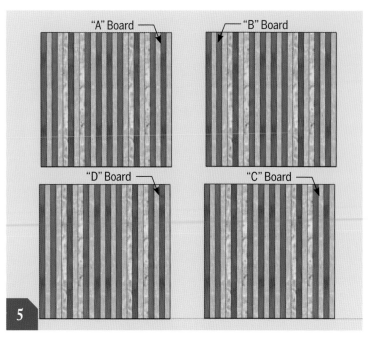

5

Lamination resawn into thinner sections

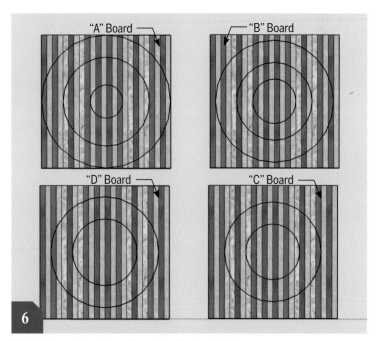

6

Ring information transferred to the laminations

such as cutting every second ring or third ring from one board.

Label the layers that can be cut from the same laminated board in sequential order such as "A", "B", "C", etc.

Make a lamination of multi-colored woods. The woods should be planed or sanded to flatness so that the glue up will be perfect. It may be easier to assemble multiple small sections and then combine those into a larger lamination. The width of the lamination must equal or exceed the diameter of the project. Where multiple boards are needed, make the lamination's length twice the desired project diameter so it can be cut in half to yield two laminations *(Figure 4)*

Laminations made from ¾" stock can easily be split into thinner sections and planed or sanded smooth yielding more laminates for the project. *(Figure 5)*

Prepare the Rings

From your drawing transfer the dimensions of "A" layers to the "A" board with a compass and label each one. Similarly do the same for each other board required for your project. *(Figure 6)*

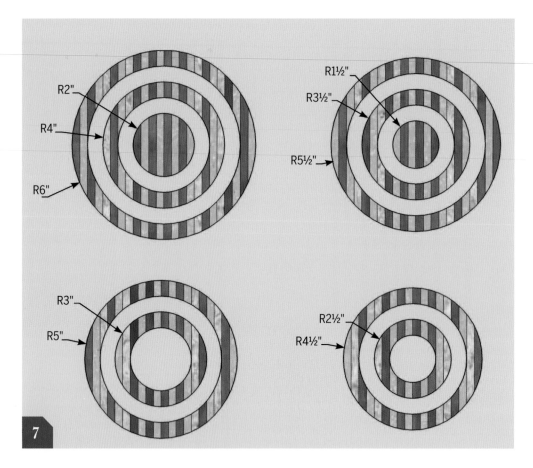

R2"
R4"
R6"
R1½"
R3½"
R5½"

Rings separated

7

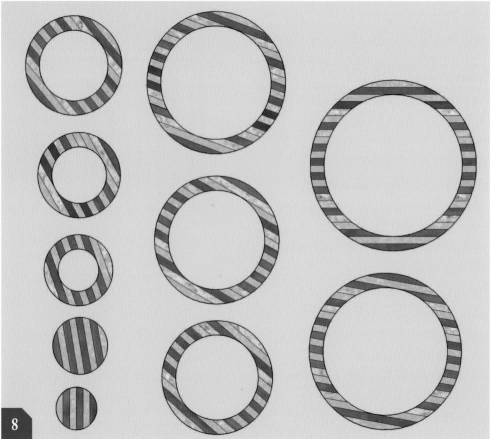

R3"
R5"
R2½"
R4½"

Rings in order ready for assembly

8

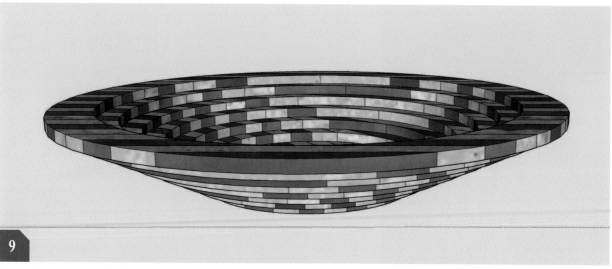

9

Ring all glued up ready to turn

10

Using a laminated block

Cut the ring free from the boards keeping each properly labeled for later assembly. *(Figure 7)*

Arrange the rings in the sequence for assembly and begin the glue up process. *(Figure 8)*

Build the vessel starting with a solid foot and adding one ring at a time. As you glue on each ring rotate it a measured amount then glue it into place. *(Figure 9)*

For some smaller projects a laminated block can be purchased and re-sawn into the needed layers, as is show here. *(Photo 10)*

11

Slicing a laminated block

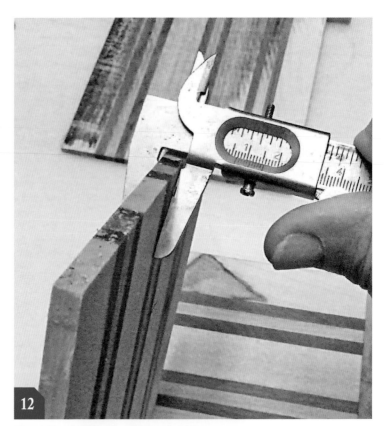

12

Check the thickness of the laminations

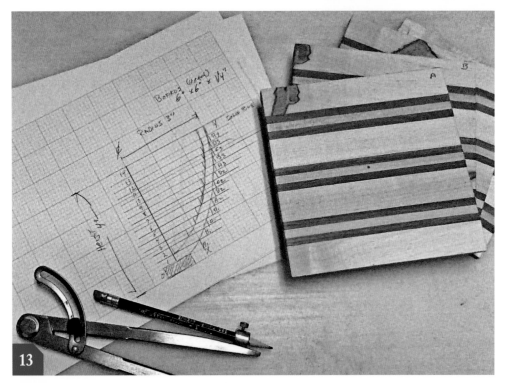

13

Using the drawing to mark the layers on the boards

The block is converted into thin laminations by re-sawing into ⅜". *(Photo 11)* After sawing, the slices are sanded flat and sized to a constant ¼" dimension. *(Photo 12)*

Prepare a drawing for the desired vessel. A bowl form was drawn on graph paper, ¼" layers are marked and non-overlapping circles drawn. This project will require four laminated boards due to its shape. *(Photo 13)* Each board was labeled individually "A," "B," "C," & "D" and the drawing was marked the same.

Laying out the circles. The boards were marked by transferring the outside radius of each layer to the appropriate board. *(Photos 14 and 15)*

Measuring the drawing with a compass

Transferring the dimensions to a board

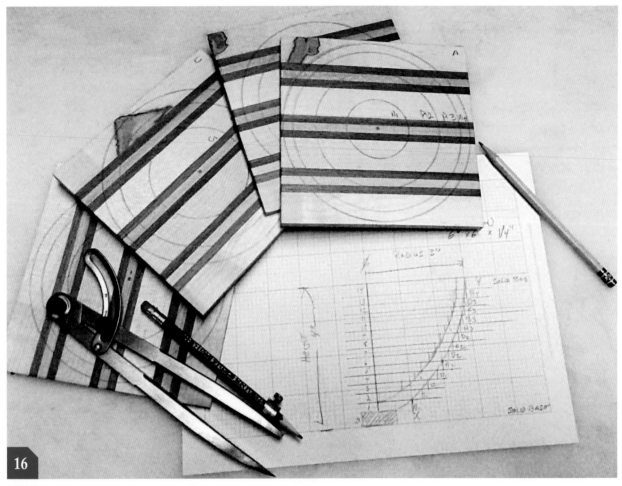

16

Boards ready to cut

17

Layer mounted ready to part off rings

When all the circles are transferred, the boards are ready to be cut into rings. *(Photo 16)*

Cutting the rings. A faceplate was prepared with a large flat sacrificial board attached. After trimming the corners of each laminated board, it is clamped to the faceplate at its center. *(Photo 17)*

Each ring is parted off at the marked line using a thin parting tool and cutting at an inward 45-degree angle. The outer ring is separated first. Since it will remain captured due to the cutting angle it is taped down to the faceplate to prevent its flopping around before the next inner ring is parted free. *(Photo 18)*

When all the rings have been parted free, be certain that each is correctly labeled and placed in assembly order. *(Photo 19)*

18

Parting off a ring

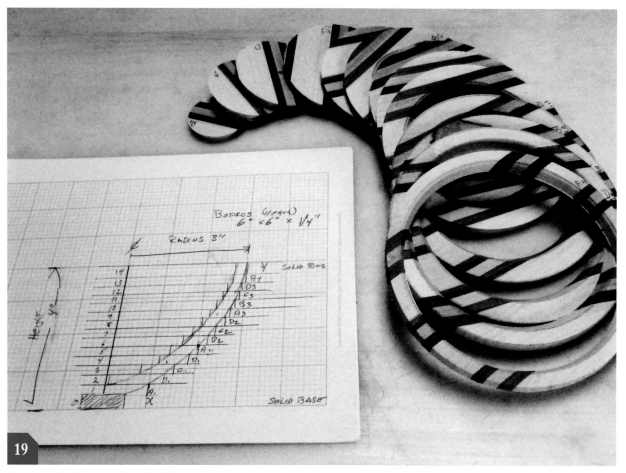

19

Rings labeled and ready to build

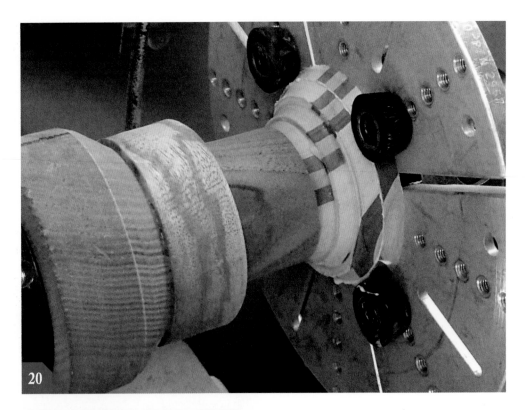

Gluing on a ring

Building the vessel. On the project faceplate/glue block start the assembly in sequence rotating each added ring a fixed amount before gluing into place. *(Photo 20)*

When all the rings are glued in place, complete the vessel with a solid contrasting top ring. *(Photo 21)*

Turn the vessel. A support cone may be necessary for larger, unstable projects. *(Photo 22)*

After the turning is completed, reduce the base, sand and add a topcoat. *(Photo 23)*

Part off and complete the bottom of the foot. *(Photo 24)*

Completed assembly with a solid base and top ring

22 Turning the vessel

23 Bowl shaped and ready to finish

24 Completed project

8

Other Ideas— Segmented Pens

1

A segmented pen

Segmented pens are easy projects that make great gifts and conversation pieces.

In this illustration *(Photo 1)* a standard 7mm pen kit available from many suppliers is used. Other kits also can be adapted by drilling the correct diameter hole and preparing enough material for the needed barrel length. Refer to the instruction sheet supplied with your kit for more information.

Careful preparation requires accurate milling of the wood to assure tight glue joints. Making thin slices of the glued up blanks will require a table saw with a zero clearance insert to prevent the loss of the slices.

Materials required:

- Pen kit (7 mm kits have 2 each 2⅛" brass tubes).
- Two contrasting wood species milled to ½" square and 24" in length minimum.
- PVA glue for gluing up the wood strips.

2

First glue up

- Thin cyanoacrylate glue for adhering the thin sections.
- Medium CA glue to start the slices.
- Lots of clamps.
- Drill bits (for this kit you will need 7 mm drills).
- Gloves for use when applying glue.

Cut two species of wood to ½" square and a minimum of 24" in length. Mill smooth, glue and clamp. *(Photo 2)*

When the glue is dry, cross cut the strip in half, clean surfaces and re-glue the two sections reversing the colors. *(Photo 3)*

When the glue is dry, clean up the re-glued strip and assure that it remains square. *(Photo 4)*

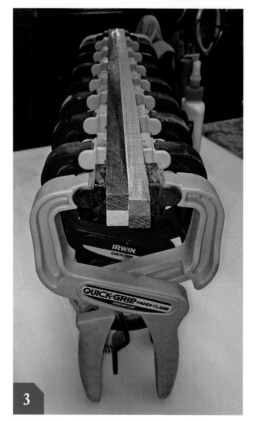

3

Second glue up

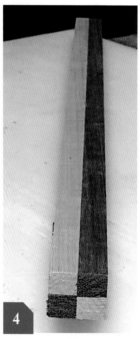

4

Blank cleaned up and ready to drill

Starting drilling with a short drill bit

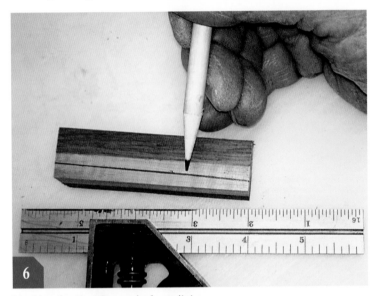

Marking for the glue up before slicing

Cutting thin slices

Cut the square stock into shorter sections that can be drilled. If you choose to drill with a longer drill bit, start the hole with a stubbier one, then change bits halfway through. *(Photo 5)*

After completing the drilling, mark a pencil line on one face of the light colored species ⅛" from the edge before cutting the stock into slices. This will be used later for marking the rotation during assembly. *(Photo 6)*

Prepare a cutting sled to safely slice thin sections. Use a 60-80-tooth finish blade. The blade must be sharp to get clean surfaces. *(Photo 7)*

Slice enough thin sections ⅛" to 3⁄16" thick for each brass tube. Remember that you lose ⅛" width with each saw kerf. Sand each cut face. *(Photo 8)*

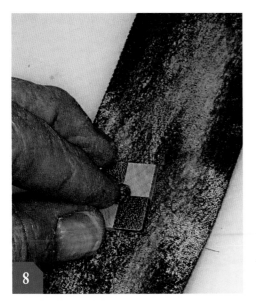

8

Sanding the slices

9

Roughing the brass

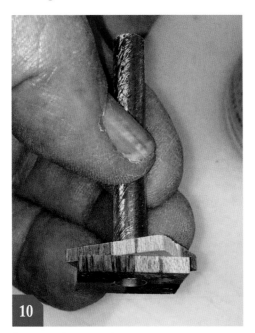

10

Starting the assembly

11

First set of slices assembled

Rough the surface of each brass tube with 60-80 grit sandpaper to increase the "tooth" for the glue up. *(Photo 9)*

With nitrile gloves on, add the first slice to the end of the first brass tube with medium CA glue. Assure that it is well attached, square to the tube, and the glue is dry.

Place the second slice on the same tube using the pencil line to rotate this slice a specific amount. *(Photo 10)*

With the thin CA glue tack one corner of the added slice in place. Repeat this step with each additional slice until the brass tube is filled. *(Photo 11)*

12 Saturating the assembly with CA glue

13 Turning the pen blanks

14 All the steps in
the process

Lay the completed glue up on its side on a protected surface and flood it with the thin CA glue. Rotate the tube 90 degrees and flood it again. This will lock all the slices into permanent place. *(Photo 12)*

Sand the ends of the tubes square until the shiny ends of the brass tubes are visible.

Assemble the two blanks on the pen mandrel and carefully turn the blanks round. Finally, complete the desired shape and sand. *(Photo 13)*

Finish the turned blanks with a friction polish, spray lacquer or a CA finish. Penetrating oil finish is not recommended, as it won't penetrate the CA glue used for assembly.

Assemble the pen as described in the kit instruction sheet. *(Photo 14)*

Other Ideas— Transitional Vessels

9

Transitional vessels are simple constructions which only include one or two segmented rings with a body of solid hardwoods. These fun projects can be constructed from scrap woods and pen blanks. The process follows standard construction on two faceplates. If the feature ring is of appropriate thickness and width it can be cored and split on the lathe so that several vessels could be built from one ring glue up.

Mini transitional vessels

Stack of stock

Select Materials from Your Scrap

Cut a rectangle of burl wood or other quality stock into sections for the top and bottom generally divided at ¼ and ¾ of its height.

Select materials for the vessel base and top about ½ the diameter of the above stock and contrasting woods.

Cut veneers into squares to fit between the layers and add any other decorative components from available scrap. *(Photo 1)*

Measure the stock to determine the feature ring diameter and build a ring from a contrasting stock or pen blank scraps. You can determine the segment edge length from the Segment Edge Estimation Table in the appendix and avoid all calculations *(Photo 2)*

Build the vessel on two faceplates as in other projects. Base to feature ring on one faceplate and the top down on the other.

Hollow the base section only enough so that the feature ring can be attached only to the desired wall thickness; allowing the interior portion to be easily cored out and used for another project. *(Photo 3)*

Glue on the feature ring. *(Photo 4)*

Feature ring made from pen blanks

Base hollowed ready to mount the feature ring

Glue on the feature ring

Splitting the feature ring

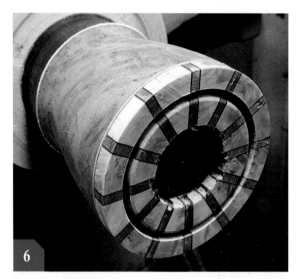

Coring the feature ring

After truing up, the feature ring can be split into two separate rings. *(Photo 5)*

Since the feature ring was only glued at its outer rim, the interior can also be cored free for another project. *(Photo 6)*

In this project the cored feature ring is used to start building the top section of the vessel. *(Photo 7)*

Feature ring core used to start the top of the vessel

Top portion of the vessel built

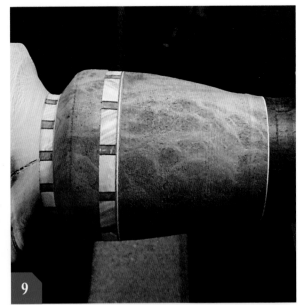

Shaping the exterior

Hollow and seal the interiors

Glue the halves together

The top portion of the vessel is assembled and flattened ready to shape the full exterior. Note the use of veneers between the layers. *(Photo 8)*

Clamp the two flattened halves together and shape the exterior but leave the base oversized for additional support. *(Photo 9)*

Hollow the interiors of the halves and seal them with shellac or other appropriate sealer. *(Photo 10)*

Glue the halves together. When the glue is dry, clean off any remaining glue from the exterior and part the neck portion free from its glue block. *(Photo 11)*

Re-true the exterior if necessary and complete the neck area. Lastly

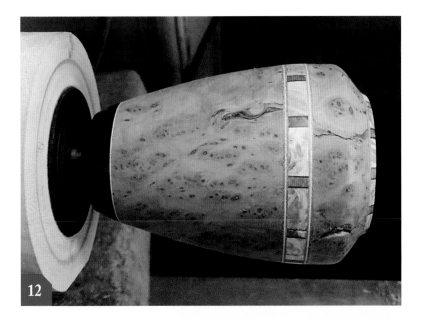

Completing
the exterior

Parting cut added and ready for top coat

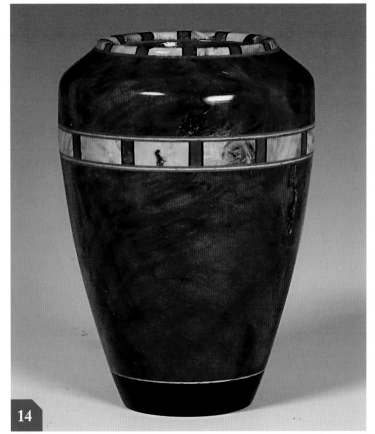

The finished vessel

reduce the base diameter to the finished dimension. *(Photo 12)*

Add a narrow parting cut to the bottom of the base before completing the sanding and top coating of the exterior. *(Photo 13)*

Part off the project and complete the bottom of the base using a jam or vacuum chuck. *(Photo 14)*

Appendix

Sources and Site References

Sources of Software Useful in Segmented Turning

Integrated software for design and layout in one program

- http://www.segmentedturning.com/software.htm

Programs separated for shape design, project planning, and laminate construction

- http://woodturnerpro.com/

Source for pen and paper planning tools and software for your cell phone

- http://turnedwood.com/

Live Centers and Support Cones

Live center systems designed to support chucks and alignment cones

- Oneway or Jet live center systems and matching lathe thread adapters

Auxiliary alignment cones that attach to the above live centers with a ¾ x 10 thread

- Solid aluminum cone: http://www.segmentedturning.com/Frustum.htm
- Aluminum cone slightly hollowed: http://www.curttheobald.com/store.html
- High density plastic set of three sizes: http://advancedlathetools.com/atlwebhome_006.htm

Oneway live center and alignment cones

Wedgie Sled™ Materials

Plans and video on constructing the sled

- http://segeasy.com/wedgiesledplan1.pdf

Wedgies for setting included segment angles

- 30-60-90 triangle from a local office supply store for 12 segment rings
- Wedgies for other segmented rings: http://segeasy.com/toystore2.htm

Open Segment Accessories

Commercial indexing plates

- Aluminum plates with magnetic base for any lathe: http://alisam.com/page/14g9e/Woodworking_turning_OT.html
- Plastic, inexpensive and accurate plate: http://www.ironfirellc.com/

Printable indexing templates for making your own indexing wheel

- http://segmentedwoodturners.org/forum/TOC.php (requires membership in the organization)
- http://jlrodgers.com/EdResources/Bill%20Smith%20Files/

Plans for constructing a vertical fixture for assembly

- http://finewoodnthings.com/open_segment_glue_up_2.htm

Plans for constructing an on-lathe assembly fixture

- http://segmentedwoodturners.org/assets/bill_smith_files/

Adapter for attaching your faceplates to vertical assembly fixtures

- www.finewoodnthings.com

Plans and instructions for building a Segment Stomper

- http://woodturnerpro.com/content.php?r=190-Segment-Stomper-Details

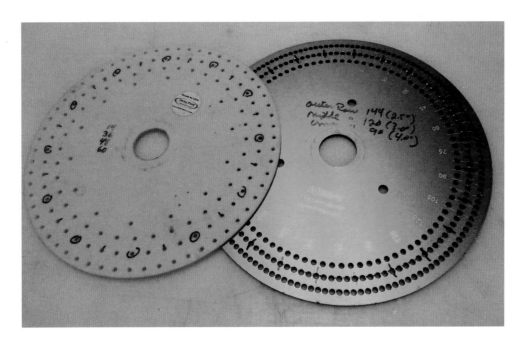

Commercial indexing plates

Building a Table Saw 15 Degree Segment Cutting Sled

Here is one plan for building a fixed-angle cutting sled for your table saw. Other angles can be constructed but the segment fence will be committed to one specific ring. Information on how to calculate the dimensions for other cutting angles is at the end of this description.

Cut the following stock to dimensions

- 1 each 18" x 24" x ½" plywood or Melamine cut dead square.
- 2 each ½" x ¾" x 24"strips for miter groove guides or commercial miter slot guides can be used.
- 1 each ¾" x 3" x 24" hardwood segment fence.
- 1 each 2" x 4" x 24" rear cross support brace.
- 1 each 2" x 2" x 24" front cross support fence.

Purchase the following additional supplies

- 2 each 1½" bolts with head diameter less than ¾" with washers and nuts.

- Wood screws 1".
- ¾" Forstner bit.
- Wood glue.
- Toggle clamp with ¾" mounting screws.
- One each stick-on measuring tape (Right Hand).
- Fine ink pen.
- Square.
- Vernier calipers.

Assemble sled

- Be sure the 18" x 24" base is smooth on both sides; sanding may be needed.
- Place miter guides in table saw miter slots on top of spacers to raise them above table saw surface.

Classical fixed angle sled

- Bring the table saw's fence to a 12" setting and lock in place.
- Place glue on the miter guides and set the 18"x 24"sled base on top and abutted to the saw's fence to square it.
- Add weight and allow glue to dry.

Add cross supports

- Carefully align front and back 2" x 4" x 24" cross support braces with the front and rear edges for the sled base.
- Glue and clamp them and allow the glue to dry.

Cut saw kerf

- Clean up any glue and scrape miter slides until they are operating smoothly on the saw table. Wax the back and miter slides.
- Raise the saw blade and cut a kerf through the rear cross support and 12" into the sled. This will be the reference for setting the segment fence to its exact angle.

Mount the hardwood segment fence

- Using an accurate protractor set the sled's segment fence into place at 15 degrees relative to the saw kerf and clamp it firmly in place.
- Flip the sled over side-to-side (rear fence is still in the rear) and drill one hole in each miter guide and through the clamped 15-degree segment fence. Cut a

second shallow hole of sufficient diameter to fully recess the bolt head into the miter guide.
- The right hand hole should be about 4" from front edge of the sled and the left hand hole is 7½" from front edge.

Complete the segment fence assembly

- Turn the sled right side up and remove the segment fence and elongate one of its drilled holes in the base to ½" long.
- Bolt the segment fence in place readjusting accurately to 15 degrees with your protractor.
- Add a toggle clamp to the segment fence approximately 6 inches to the right of the saw kerf.
- Cut a short strip of hardwood with the sled to use as a segment stop.

Calibrate the sled

- Rip several test strips of hardwood to 1" width.
- Place the sled on the table saw and set the table saw blade to an accurate 90-degree vertical with a good straight edge. Measure to the bed of the cutting sled not to the table saw.
- Clamp the segment stop in place with the toggle clamp.
- Carefully cut six segments using the sled flipping the stock at each cut.
- Snugly assemble the six pieces against a straight edge. There should be no gaps between the

segment and the fence—
a 180-degree half circle.

- If there is a gap on the outside of the semicircle of segments, the angle is too acute. Loosen the bolt attaching the fence at the elongated hole and adjust the segment fence to decrease the angle. If the gap is on the inside of the semicircle, the angle is too oblique, adjust the fence in the opposite direction.
- Repeat by cutting another 6 segments and re-testing.
- When the six segments test appears perfect, cut a set of 12 segments (a full ring) and assemble it to check again for gaps. Use a bright light to locate small errors in the fence setting.
- Readjust the segment fence as needed to decrease the gaps to

zero, then screw the segment fence firmly in place with several wood screws on both sides of the saw kerf.

Completing the project

- Make a new segment stop with the newly calibrated sled. At the same time nick the new miter fence with the saw blade.
- Flip the new cut stop and clamp it so that the narrow foot of the cut aligns exactly with the nick in the fence. Clamp it firmly with the toggle clamp.
- At a convenient location on the stop, place a fine line with an ink pen and square. Align the stick-on measuring tape's 0-inch mark with the line drawn on the stop. Stick the measuring tape in place.

Trigonometry for Segmented Turners

Angle functions are useful in calculating the setup of sleds for specific angles. When accurately determined the calculations can set the segment fence precisely. The longer the measured line, the more accurate the set up will be. To calculate the proper angle, you need to use the appropriate trig function. Here they are:

Setting up a segment fence with trig

- Draw a horizontal line across the full width of the sled.
- Calculate the distance up the right hand side of the sled by using the tangent of the desired angle.
- Measure up the right hand side of the sled the exact number of inches from your calculation and mark.
- Draw a line from that mark to the beginning of the horizontal line.
- Align the sled fence to that line for the proper angle.

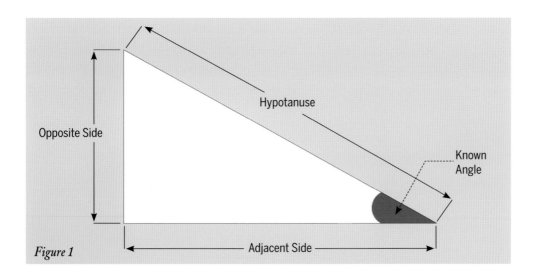

Figure 1

Angle	Sine	Cosine	Tangent
30 degrees (6 sides)	.5000	.8660	.5774
22.5 degrees (8 sides)	.3827	.9239	.4142
18 degrees (10 sides)	.3090	.9511	.3249
15 degrees (12 sides)	.2588	.9659	.2679
11.25 degrees (16 sides)	.1951	.9808	.1989
7.5 degrees (24 sides)	.1305	.9914	.1317

Sine=Opposite/Hypotenuse **Cosine=Adjacent/Hypotenuse** **Tangent=Opposite/Adjacent**

Example:

A 12-segment ring requires a 15-degree segment-cutting angle. *(Figure 2)*

Building a sled with a 24" width will require a right hand side of 6.43" from the horizontal.

The tangent 15 degrees x 24"= right-hand rise dimension.

0.2679 x 24" = 6.43"

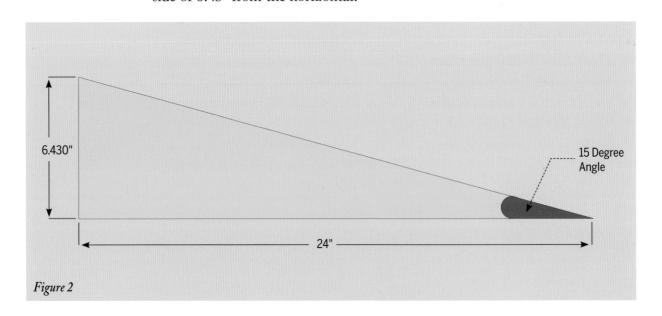

6.430"

15 Degree Angle

24"

Figure 2

Zero Clearance Insert for the Miter Sled and the Wedgie Sled™

It is important that the segments fall away from the cutting blade as they are being cut. To insure this, build a new insert for your table saw with a segment deflector.

- Purchase or make a blank insert for your table saw.
- Carefully clamp the insert into position with the edge of the fence system and raise the blade through it with the power turned on to cut a perfect zero clearance slot.
- Remove the insert and glue a length of quarter round molding or a 45-degree wedge partially over the blade slot.
- Replace the insert in the saw and repeat the cutting by clamping the insert and raising the powered blade.
- Sand any burrs and smooth the surfaces.

Use this insert every time you cut on a miter sled or the Wedgie Sled to allow the segments to be moved away from the spinning blade.

Segment Stop

Using a miter sled or the SegEasy sled requires a stop to measure to the length of the cut off (the piece that is the segment). This is one way to build this stop. Other stops can be built to fit over the saw's miter fence.

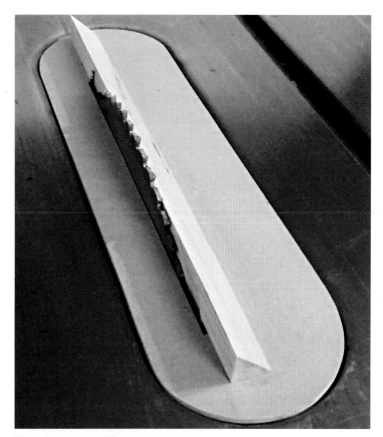

Zero clearance table saw insert

Segment Stop

Segment Edge Determination Table

Ring dia.	Number of segments planned per ring				
	6 segments	8 segments	12 segments	16 segments	24 segments
1"	⁹/₁₆	⁷/₁₆	¼	³/₁₆	⅛
1.5"	⅞	⅝	⅜	⁵/₁₆	³/₁₆
2	1⅛	¹³/₁₆	⁹/₁₆	⅜	¼
2.5	1⁷/₁₆	1¹/₁₆	¹¹/₁₆	½	⁵/₁₆
3.0	1¾	1¼	¹³/₁₆	⅝	⅜
3.5	2	1⁷/₁₆	¹⁵/₁₆	¹¹/₁₆	⁷/₁₆
4.0	2⁵/₁₆	1¹¹/₁₆	1¹/₁₆	¹³/₁₆	½
4.5	2⅝	1⅞	1³/₁₆	⅞	⁹/₁₆
5.0	2⅞	2¹/₁₆	1⁵/₁₆	1	¹¹/₁₆
5.5	3³/₁₆	2¼	1½	1⅛	¾
6.0	3⁷/₁₆	2½	1⅝	1³/₁₆	¹³/₁₆
6.5	3¾	2¹¹/₁₆	1¾	1⁵/₁₆	⅞
7.0	4¹/₁₆	2⅞	1⅞	1⅜	¹⁶/₁₆
7.5	4⁵/₁₆	3⅛	2	1½	1
8.0	4⅝	3⁵/₁₆	2⅛	1⁹/₁₆	1¹/₁₆
8.5	4¹⁵/₁₆	3½	2¼	1¹¹/₁₆	1⅛
9.0	5³/₁₆	3¾	2⁷/₁₆	1¹³/₁₆	1³/₁₆
9.5	5½	3¹⁵/₁₆	2⁹/₁₆	1⅞	1¼
10.0	5¾	4⅛	2¹¹/₁₆	2	1⁵/₁₆
10.5	6¹/₁₆	4⅜	2¹³/₁₆	2¹/₁₆	1⅜
11.0	6⅜	4⁹/₁₆	2¹⁵/₁₆	2³/₁₆	1⁷/₁₆
11.5	6⅝	4¾	3¹/₁₆	2⁵/₁₆	1½
12.0	6¹⁵/₁₆	5	3³/₁₆	2⅜	1⁹/₁₆
12.5	7³/₁₆	5³/₁₆	3⅜	2½	1⅝
13.0	7½	5⅜	3½	2⁹/₁₆	1¹¹/₁₆
13.5	7¹³/₁₆	5⁹/₁₆	3⅜	2¹¹/₁₆	1¾
14.0	8¹/₁₆	5¹³/₁₆	3¾	2 ¹³/₁₆	1¹³/₁₆
14.5	8⅜	6	3⅞	2⅞	1¹⁵/₁₆
15.0	8¹¹/₁₆	6³/₁₆	4	3	2
15.5	8¹⁵/₁₆	8⁷/₁₆	4⅛	3¹/₁₆	2¹/₁₆
16.0	9¼	6⅝	4⁵/₁₆	3³/₁₆	2¹/₁₆
16.5	9½	6 ¹³/₁₆	4⁷/₁₆	3⁵/₁₆	2³/₁₆
17.0	9¹³/₁₆	7¹/₁₆	4⁹/₁₆	3⅜	2 ¼
17.5	10⅛	7¼	4¹¹/₁₆	3½	2⁵/₁₆
18.0	10⅜	7⁷/₁₆	4¹³/₁₆	3⁹/₁₆	2⅜
18.5	10¹¹/₁₆	7¹¹/₁₆	4¹⁵/₁₆	3¹¹/₁₆	2⅞
19.0	11	7⅞	5¹/₁₆	3¾	2½
19.5	11¼	8¹/₁₆	5¼	3⅞	2⁹/₁₆
20.0	11⁹/₁₆	5⅝	5⅜	4	2⅝

Imperial/Metric Conversions

Imperial (inches)	Decimal inches	Metric (centimeters)
1/16	0.0625	0.1587
1/8	0.125	0.3175
3/16	0.1875	.476
1/4	.250	.635
5/16	.3125	.794
3/8	.375	.952
7/16	.4375	1.111
1/2	.500	1.270
9/16	.5625	1.429
5/8	.625	1.587
11/16	.6875	1.746
3/4	.750	1.905
13/16	.8125	2.064
7/8	.875	2.222
15/16	.9375	2.381
1	1.000	2.54
2	2.000	5.08
3	3.000	7.62
4	4.000	10.16
5	5.000	12.70
6	6.000	15.24
7	7.000	17.78
8	8.000	30.32
9	9.000	22.86
10	10.000	25.40
11	11.000	27.94
12	12.000	30..48
24	24.000	60.96
36	36.000	91.44
48	48.000	121.92
60	60.000	152.4

SIN–COS–TAN of Common Angles

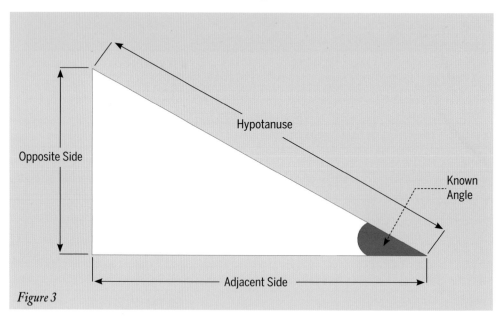

Figure 3

***Sine**=Opposite/Hypotenuse* ***Cosine**=Adjacent/Hypotenuse* ***Tangent**=Opposite/Adjacent*

Angle (degrees)	SIN	COS	TAN
5	.08716	.9962	.0875
10	.1734	.9848	.1763
12.5	.2164	.9763	.2217
15	.2588	.9569	.2679
22.5	.3827	.9239	.4142
30	.5000	.8660	.5773
45	.7071	.7071	1.000
60	.8660	.5000	1.7320
75	.9659	.2588	3.7320
90	1.000	0000	Error

Glossary of Segment Terms

BFB (Bowl from a Board)	An assembly technique using wood lamination cut into rings and assembled with rotation between assembled rings. See chapter 7.	Seal Coat	A top coat applied specifically to seal the wood and may precede a final finish.
Complementary segments	Two segments are considered complementary if their combined angles, though different, add up to the combined angle of two regular identical segments.	SegEasy™	A trade name of Jerry Bennett's line of products for attaching open segments to a project.
Compound Staves	Tall segments cut at a compound angle to minimize the usage of materials.	Segment	A single piece of wood cut to a specific angle for assembly into rings.
Cut Angle	One half of the segment included angle.	Segment Stomper	An adaptation of the SegEasy™ plates that allows for accurate centering of the applied ring to the project.
Dizzy Bowl	See BFB (Bowl from a Board).	Segment Stop	A table saw accessory to measure the amount of cutoff from a miter-style sled.
Driskell Fixture	A vertical fixture used in assembling open segment projects.	Smith Fixture	The on-lathe fixture initially proposed for open segment construction by Bill Smith in 2002.
Floating foot	A technique to eliminate fractures from wood movement in vessel feet. Similar to stile and rail cabinet construction	Stave Segment Construction	Tall segments used for vessel construction with one or two rings.
Greek Key feature	A square pattern created by flipping laminations and intermixing with matching spacers in ring construction.	"T" Bird (Thunderbird)	A sliced design assembly. See chapter 5.
Included angle	The segment angle equal to 360 degrees divided by the number of segments in the planned ring.	Top Coat	The finish coat applied to the complete project for protection and beauty.
Indexing plates	A plate that will fit a lathe's headstock divided into degrees of rotation for placing segments in open segment constructions.	Traditional Sled	A fix-angle miter style sled made for cutting a single segment angle very accurately.
Miter Sled	An adjustable table saw sled system for cutting angles on the end of a strip of wood.	Veneers	Thin slices of wood which may be stained. Used in segmented turning for emphasis and separation.
Open Segment Construction	A process of mounting individual segments at fixed radial positions creating gaps in the assembly.	Wedgies™	Fixed-angle plates used to set the included angles for the Wedgie Sleds.
PVA glue	Poly Vinyl Acetate wood glue such as the Titebond™ family.	Wedgie Sled™	A two-fence system for cutting accurate segments on the table saw. Introduced in 2013 by Jerry Bennett.
Ring Segment Construction	A technique using segmented rings to build a bowl or vessel. See chapters 1 and 3.	Zero Clearance Insert	A table saw blade insert with no space between the blade and the insert. Protects against the loss of small cutoffs.

More Great Woodworking Books from Linden Publishing

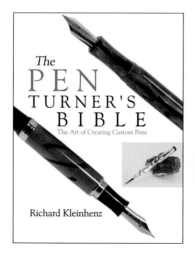

The Pen Turner's Bible
152 pp. $22.95
978-0-941936-61-3

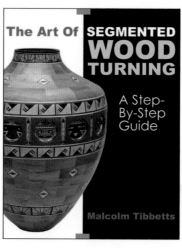

Art of Segmented Woodturning
200 pp. $25.95
978-0-941936-86-6

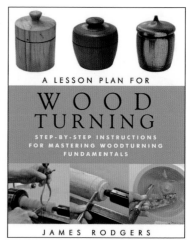

A Lesson Plan for Woodturning
112 pp. $19.95
978-1-610351-81-2

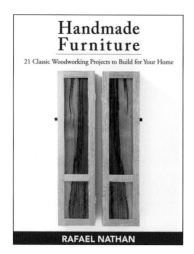

Handmade Furniture
112 pp. $19.95
978-1-610352-10-9

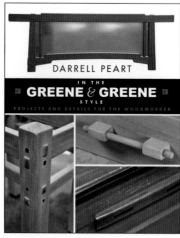

In the Greene & Greene Style
128 pp. $24.95
978-1-610351-80-5

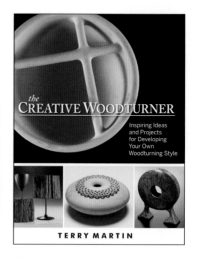

The Creative Woodturner
144 pp. $24.95
978-1-610352-18-5

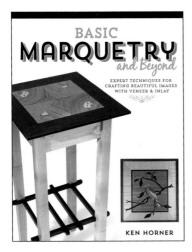

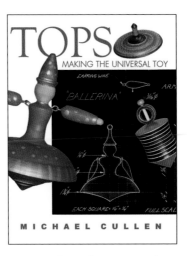
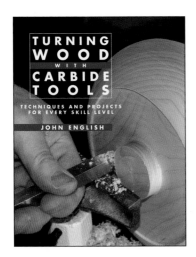

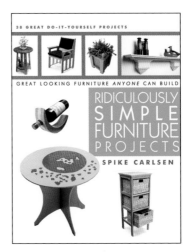

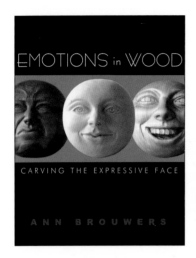
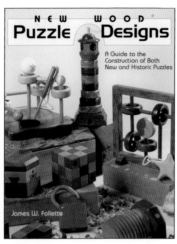
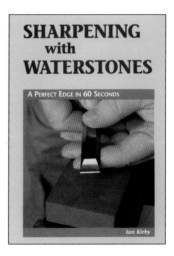
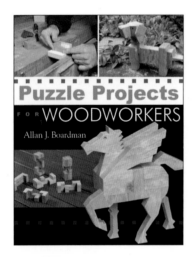
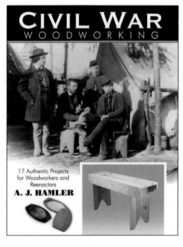
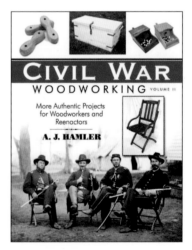